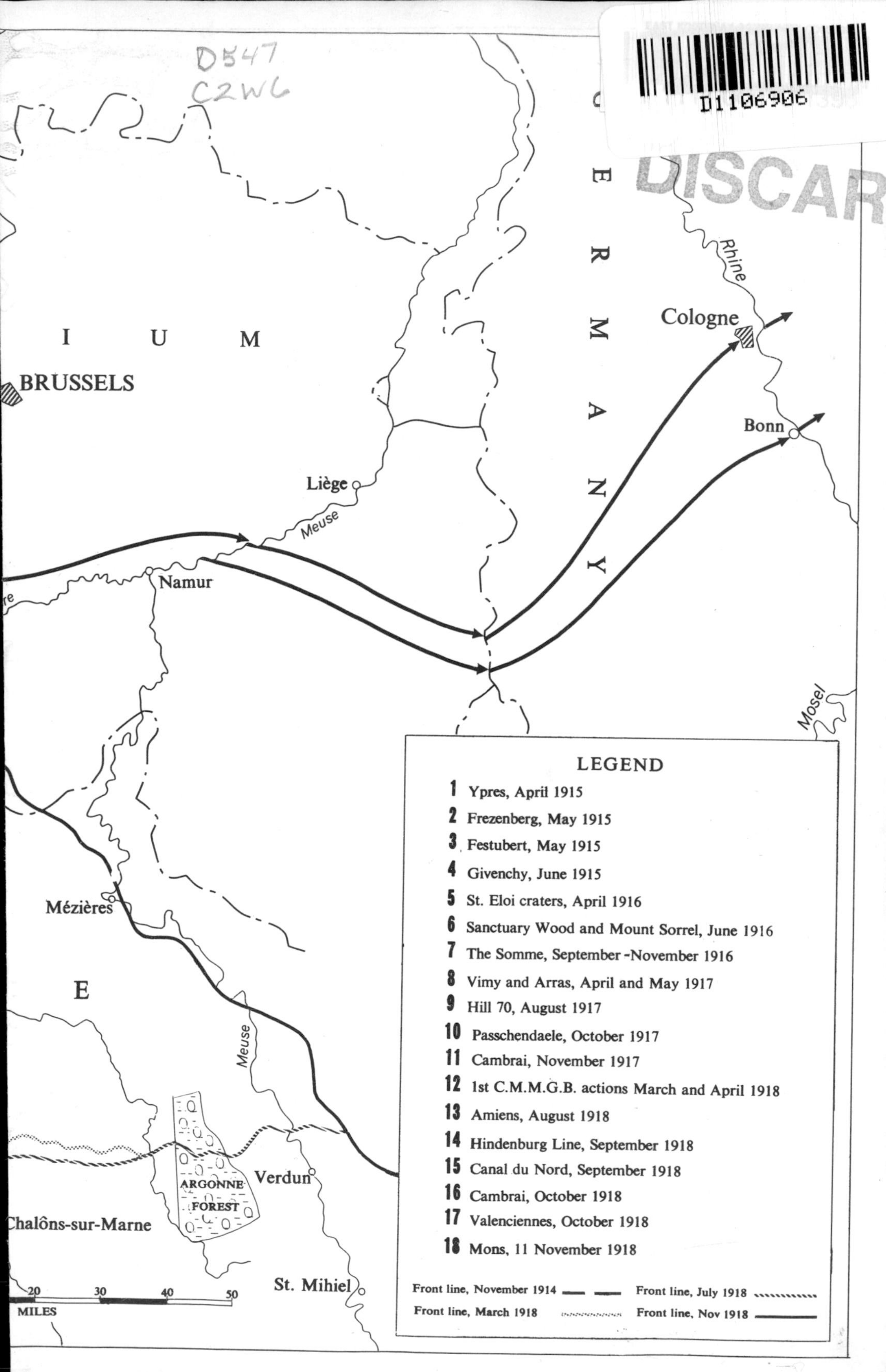
GERMANY
IUM
BRUSSELS
Cologne
Rhine
Bonn
Liège
Meuse
Namur
Mosel
Mézières
E
Meuse
ARGONNE FOREST
Verdun
Chalôns-sur-Marne
St. Mihiel
20 30 40 50
MILES
LEGEND
1 Ypres, April 1915
2 Frezenberg, May 1915
3 Festubert, May 1915
4 Givenchy, June 1915
5 St. Eloi craters, April 1916
6 Sanctuary Wood and Mount Sorrel, June 1916
7 The Somme, September -November 1916
8 Vimy and Arras, April and May 1917
9 Hill 70, August 1917
10 Passchendaele, October 1917
11 Cambrai, November 1917
12 1st C.M.M.G.B. actions March and April 1918
13 Amiens, August 1918
14 Hindenburg Line, September 1918
15 Canal du Nord, September 1918
16 Cambrai, October 1918
17 Valenciennes, October 1918
18 Mons, 11 November 1918
Front line, November 1914
Front line, July 1918
Front line, March 1918
Front line, Nov 1918

WA

TRAIL. B.C.

amid the guns below

LARRY WORTHINGTON

amid the guns below

THE STORY OF THE CANADIAN CORPS

(1914-1919)

McCLELLAND AND STEWART LIMITED
TORONTO/MONTREAL

The Canadian Publishers
McClelland and Stewart Limited
25 Hollinger Road, Toronto 16.

PRINTED AND BOUND IN CANADA
BY JOHN DEYELL LTD., LINDSAY

contents

author's note

I was not yet in my teens when the First World War broke out. My father was an Englishman and a Quaker. The war distressed him greatly and its depressive effects contributed to his death in 1918.

At home and at school we followed the progress of the war closely; watched the grown-ups turn first to the daily casualty lists in the newspapers as they now turn to the comics and the stock market reports; wept with our English teacher when she recited "In Flanders Fields." It was an impressionable age, and later when I married a man who had been through some of it, and listened to stories of "old sweats," the impression was a lasting one.

As the fiftieth anniversary of the start of World War I approached, a flux of books on the subject appeared, but none I have read has done more than mention that Canada also participated. Colonel Nicholson's excellent official history, *Canadian Expeditionary Force 1914-1919*, published in 1962, pays high tribute to the Canadians and their Corps Commander at the conclusion of his book, but it is too easily missed. I wish he had made it at the beginning instead.

I had no idea, however, of writing a book on the subject, even after Dr. Mark Marshall of Edmonton, an original with the 1st Motor Machine Gun Brigade, asked if I would consider writing a history of the Machine Gun Corps. But in the fall of 1963 I acquired transcripts of tape-recorded recollections made that year by Brigadier General Raymond Brutinel, commander of both the Canadian Motor Machine Gun Brigade and the Canadian Machine Gun Corps in the First World War. The general, then eighty-one and living in France, felt that the Canadian Corps in general, the machine-gunners in particular, had never received the recognition in their own country that they deserved. It was his fervent wish that this be remedied, and I recognized here the source of Dr. Marshall's query, for the general had been his commander from the first, and had remained a close and valued friend.

Urged on by the general, Dr. Marshall, and Mr. A. E. Powley, who had interviewed Brutinel at length for a Canadian Broadcasting Corporation program, as well as by my husband, an old machine-gunner himself, I reluctantly started work, unsure of my capabilities, with only a little knowledge and few preconceived ideas.

After a couple of false starts my reluctance vanished. Research showed that the Canadian Corps had indeed been outstanding, their achievements for a small force spectacular, earning admiration and respect from Allied armies as well as the enemy. I, too, soon shared the general's desire to see the Corps and its commander, General Sir Arthur Currie, take an honoured place in Canadian history.

By the late spring of 1964 I had the first rough draft of the manuscript ready, and Dr. Marshall took it to France and read it to the general, now eighty-two, nearly blind and in failing health. But his mind was still clear and keen, and his comments and suggestions were incorporated into the revised manuscript which he never heard. He died on September 21, 1964, at his home, Le Couloumé, near the Pyrenees. There he was buried, where so many of his Canadian countrymen had visited him, his grave marked by the same simple headstone used for all Commonwealth war graves, but with the distinguishing Canadian maple leaf.

My correspondence with the general for nearly a year was a happy feature of the work, for his letters reflected his personal charm, and I sincerely mourned his death.

In the following pages the source of General Foch's opinions is General Brutinel, who acted as liaison between the Generalissimo and General Currie. After the war the two soldiers became close friends, fighting the battles over again by the fireside. Other sources have been eye-witness accounts, and I am most grateful for having them given me.

The staff at the Army Historical Section have helped me a great deal, supplying or recommending reading material and checking the manuscript. I am particularly grateful to Colonel H. F. Wood, the Director, for all his help, and to Major C. C. J. Bond, Historian with the National Capital Commission, for the excellent map, and for his many valuable suggestions.

The encouragement and interest of Dr. Marshall, Mr. Powley, Colonel W. E. Harris of London, Ontario, and Mr. Walter Herbert of the Canada Foundation, Ottawa, are deeply appreciated.

But without the help of my husband, Worthy, the book would probably never have been written. Although I have done my own reading and research, he has interpreted army terms, helped phrase military actions, advised, praised and, not least, endured neglect and my irritable fatigue with endearing forbearance. To him, my thanks and love.

LDW
Ottawa

foreword

This is the story of the Canadian Corps in the First World War. It is nearly half a century since the end of that terrible conflict and few people today, least of all Canadians, know the facts about Canada's contribution and achievements.

The Canadian Army Corps in that war became the finest military force in Canada's history. By 1918 it surpassed, for its size, anything on the Western Front, and was recognized by the professionals as the equal of the best Allied formations.

It was only four divisions strong, but from 1917 on, it never lost a gun, never lost ground, and never failed in any assignment, although its tasks became more and more difficult. It revolutionized the tactics and employment of the machine-gun, and its complement included the first fully contained motorized armoured fighting unit in the Allied Forces—a motor machine-gun brigade. It led the Allies in advanced and effective artillery techniques. Finally, when chosen by Generalissimo Foch to spearhead the attack against the Germans in the late summer of 1918, it met and decisively defeated sixty-four fresh or rested German divisions in the last hundred days of the war. David Lloyd George in his war memoirs wrote: "Wherever the Germans found the Canadian Corps coming into the line they prepared for the worst!"

In the four years of World War I Canada, with a population of slightly more than seven million, raised a force of over 600,000 men, most of them volunteers. Of these nearly 233,000 were casualties, 59,544 fatal. These figures include all services in several theatres of war where Canadians served with distinction; the Royal Flying Corps, the Royal Navy, and services such as Engineers, Tunnellers, Forestry, railway troops and medical personnel. But the Canadian Army Corps represented the bulk of Canada's contribution. Although not part of the Corps, actions of the Canadian Cavalry Brigade are included in this narrative, for, mounted and dismounted, they fought frequently under Corps command.

The Corps was unique in that it was an amateur army. The First Contingent, over 30,000 strong, was made up predominantly of men from the British Isles, many of whom had seen service in the Imperial army or navy. But its officers were Canadian militiamen, with a sprinkling of Imperials who were on loan at the time to guide and nurture Canada's infant regular force. Succeeding divisions were composed of men from all walks of life—doctors, lawyers, scholars, labourers, farmers, fishermen, miners and certainly not least, schoolboys, thousands of them destined never to grow old.

The First Contingent left Canada early in October 1914, and six months later the 1st Division was in action in France. With neither preparation nor protection it was soon to face an ordeal that was as new and terrible then as nuclear weapons seem today—gas. To the amazement of the professionals, friend and foe alike, they stood fast, and according to a War Office communiqué, "undoubtedly saved the situation." The incredible courage and recourcefulness of the 1st Division in those April days of 1915 set a standard and tradition that subsequent divisions maintained throughout the war.

The amateurs had proved they were brave. They went on to prove they were intelligent. They learned the art of war from battles, not books, and recognizing their mistakes, strove to correct them. Before long they were devising new means and methods. Relatively free from red tape and military dogma, brilliant scientific minds were permitted scope to improvise and create.

It was Lieutenant-Colonel A. G. L. McNaughton who introduced artillery methods and techniques superior to those of the Germans. Raymond Brutinel, a French Reserve Army officer who had emigrated to Canada in 1905, raised a motor machine-gun brigade in September 1914, took it to England, and trained it. Later he organized the Canadian Machine Gun Corps and devised techniques and employment of the machine-gun that raised it to the status of an arm intermediary between infantry and artillery.

If in the following pages the emphasis on machine-guns and Raymond Brutinel seems out of balance, it is because of the fact that such achievement was pioneered and developed within the Corps. The British and French despised the machine-gun as an inferior and ineffectual weapon. Sir Max Aitken (Lord Beaverbrook) in 1915 describes German machine-guns "spraying bullets like a watering-can" and mowing down Allied armies in the first months of the war. Yet Sir Douglas Haig, in a minute to the War Council in 1915, states: "The machine-gun is a much over-rated weapon and two per battalion is more than sufficient."

But the Germans had already made it a "machine-gun war" (as they made it a "tank war" in 1939). The Allies could win only by retaliation. For a long time the Canadians were the only force to realize this, and thanks to Brutinel, we beat the Germans at their own game.

The employment of our machine-guns was superb. In defence hardly a square yard was uncovered and, by a system of co-ordination, the massed fire could be switched by indirect methods from one area to another in a matter of minutes. This made Canadian defence deadly and explains why no ground was lost in 1917 and 1918. Offensively, a creeping barrage of overhead fire supported the infantry, and exposed flanks were protected by bullets instead of men. Eventually the British and French adopted similar tactics, but they never reached the peak performance of the Canadians.

The Corps owed its superiority to many factors. Before it was finally assigned to fight as one formation (Vimy Ridge, 1917) every division had been well blooded in battle. They were veterans who had fought, lived and learned, and their high degree of discipline had not robbed them of their native initiative and intelligence.

By 1918 the Corps was considerably larger than a British corps formation, by then decreased in size owing to the acute shortage of manpower. Instead of two weak corps, Canada concentrated on a strong enlarged one that could form several different tactical groups to fight, yet always have a reserve of fresh or rested troops. Its fire-power in artillery and machine-guns was tremendous.

Finally, the Corps had been fortunate in its commanders. Lieutenant-General Sir E. A. H. Alderson in 1914 had the stupendous job of whipping the over-enthusiastic First Contingent into shape and later, in September 1915, of forming the Canadian Corps. Lieutenant-General Sir Julian Byng succeeded General Alderson in June 1916 and considered himself fortunate in his command. The feeling was mutual, for General Byng was tremendously popular with the Canadians, and he in turn became exceedingly proud of them. Joined by the 4th Division, the Corps became a hard-hitting skilful force; their achievements culminated in the taking of Vimy Ridge in April 1917 when, for the first time, the Corps fought as a unit instead of in separate divisions assigned to the British.

In June 1917, Arthur Currie, a militiaman, took command and the Corps blossomed into the compact dedicated fighting machine that finally spearheaded the winning push against the Germans.

Under Currie the Corps won the reputation of taking so-called impregnable enemy positions, yet with proportionately lower casualties or captured Canadians. Currie, unlike some of the other generals of that time, deplored the wastage in casualties. He believed fire-power achieved more than manpower, and that skill, not slaughter won battles. At Passchendaele he wept over the losses of his men.

Major-General J. E. B. Seely, who commanded the Canadian Cavalry Brigade, wrote in his book *Adventure*: "Of all the men that I knew in nearly four years on the Western Front I think Currie was the man who took the most care of his men. Moreover, again and again he nearly brought his career to an end by bluntly refusing to do things which he was certain would result in loss of life without compensating advantage."

As for his ability, George F. G. Stanley, the military historian, writes: "A soldier without special training, with only a Canadian militia background, [Currie] won in a few short years the high esteem of professionals—an achievement without parallel in our military history."

As a Canadian, Currie could do that which neither Alderson nor Byng, as British regulars, could do—protest unsound assignments from British General Headquarters. As General Seely says, he all but refused to commit his men to useless suicidal engagements. Instead, he submitted alternate plans which the Higher Command acknowledged as superior and eventually adopted. He did refuse, to the anger and resentment of Sir Douglas Haig, to allow the Corps to be broken up and integrated with the British. Currie knew that the Corps' strength lay in its cohesion and unified action. They would not have done as well apart: furthermore, Sir Arthur had small regard for the ability of some of the British army commanders. Only in emergencies, and then on a temporary basis, did he permit employment of his divisions elsewhere.

Why then, did the exploits and achievements of the Corps go unrecognized by Canadians? There are several reasons. There were no press relation officers at that time, no radio broadcasts. Sir Douglas Haig disliked and discouraged war correspondents other than those of influential papers like the *Times* of London. Roland H. Hill, one Canadian war correspondent, says: "It will be noted no mention of Canadian troops taking part in these encounters [is permitted]. It was the policy of the British authorities not to mention even Overseas units at this time."

Censorship was strict and Canadian actions were embodied in British engagements and rarely given separate credits except at Ypres in 1915 and Vimy Ridge in 1917. Colonel Wilfred Bovey, one of Currie's staff officers, in a tribute to Sir Arthur at the time of his death, writes: "Mr. Punch forgot us at Passchendaele and Amiens. It remained for Ludendorff and Foch to attribute the credit."

We were forgotten at the March Retreat too, for the entries in Haig's diary, and his later complaint to the Canadian Minister of Militia and Defence, Major-General the Honourable S. C. Mewburn, unequivocally state that "the British Army alone and unaided by Canadian troops" withstood the German attack in March 1918. Yet the facts refute Haig's complaint. The Canadian Cavalry Brigade, mounted and dismounted, engaged the Germans gallantly, while the 1st Canadian Motor Machine Gun Brigade fought a nineteen-day running battle, both formations covering the disorganized retreat of Gough's Fifth Army.

At the end of the war when vicious insinuations were being made at home about Currie's callous indifference to the lives of his men, Sir Arthur wrote to the Prime Minister, Sir Robert Borden: "It has been intimated to me that a section of the American Press is seeking to belittle the work of Canadians, intimating that what we call 'Imperial troops' have done the bulk of the fighting. . . . English press reports on operations since August 8th [1918] have in very few cases been fair or just to Canadians. . . . Our own papers republish the English articles . . . and the Canadian people do not even now realize the full extent of the [Corps'] operation . . . and may think the casualties have been unduly heavy."

When peace was restored and censorship lifted, Canada's war correspondents told the facts, but by that time Canadians were not interested in war stories.

The Corps Commander, Arthur Currie, even before he succeeded General Byng, had made enemies of politically powerful Canadians who sought to have him removed. Sheer ability and moral courage enabled him to survive the war, but a relentless persecution was carried on for some years after the war ended. Some of the story is written in Hansard, the record of Canadian parliamentary debate, for the year 1919. It is there for all to read—libellous accusations and the feeble defence of the government of the day. In the belittling of General Currie, the glory of the force he had built and led suffered too.

In the postwar era a wave of pacifism swept the country. People were sick and weary of the heartbreak and restrictions of war. Soldiers and armies were in disrepute; the men who fought the war were confused with those who made it. But an army is only a tool and can be used by rulers as effectively to keep peace as wage war.

The good—the courage, the sacrifice, the dedication to a cause—was discarded with the bad, the greedy power-hungry opportunists that feed on war.

If they ever knew, Canadians soon forgot the epic of the Canadian Army Corps of the First War and its commander.

amid the guns below

In Flanders fields the poppies blow
Between the crosses, row on row,
        That mark our place; and in the sky
        The larks, still bravely singing, fly
Scarce heard amid the guns below.

"In Flanders Fields"
John McCrae

1

THE CANADIAN EXPEDITIONARY FORCE

To people who lived in 1914, it was Year One in an entirely new life. Nothing was ever the same again.

On Tuesday, August 4 of that year the *Ottawa Free Press* brought out several editions. Headlines in huge red and black type screamed:

BRITISH ULTIMATUM! WAR IS DECLARED!
HELL'S LET LOOSE!

In this way the citizens of Canada's capital learned shortly after eight p.m. that Britain's ultimatum to Germany had expired at midnight, Greenwich Mean Time, and that Canada too was at war.

In Ottawa crowds surged onto the streets. Men marched up and down Sparks Street singing the Marseillaise, the Maple Leaf Forever, God Save the King. Four thousand men and women collected outside the Chateau Laurier Hotel, singing, shouting, waving Union Jacks. Similar demonstrations took place across the Ottawa River in Hull, and in other cities across Canada.

It was not unexpected. For those in high places the last month had been a tense one. On June 28, the heir to the Austro-Hungarian throne, Archduke Franz Ferdinand, was assassinated in Sarajevo,

Bosnia, by a Serb. Austria, demanding retribution from the recalcitrant little country of Serbia, sent ultimatum after ultimatum demanding inordinate reparations. Germany, her powerful military machine fully equipped and restless, egged her on, setting off a chain reaction among the European nations. In accordance with existing treaties, Russia backed Serbia, France supported Russia, and Britain guaranteed Belgian neutrality.

One month from the day of the assassination, Austria-Hungary declared war on Serbia. Russia and France mobilized the following week, and Germany declared war on them both. On August 4 the German army marched into Belgium as the easiest route to invade France, ignoring Britain's ultimatum to stay out. The ultimatum expired at midnight, and the world was plunged into the first of the terrible modern wars. Italy, a signatory of the Triple Alliance with Germany and Austria, later repudiated her agreement and joined the French and British. Before peace was signed, many other countries were involved—the United States, Japan, Portugal, Turkey, Bulgaria among them—and many small states disappeared altogether.

Canadians, for the most part, had enjoyed the long lazy days of July, undisturbed by the deteriorating European situation. The young people indulged in bathing, boating, tennis and croquet, skirts modestly flapping feminine ankles while young men cavorted in white flannels, striped blazers and natty straw boaters. But even to them the last week of peace was disturbing.

Concern creased the brows of adults. Housewives started stocking up on sugar and flour. The Prime Minister, Sir Robert Borden, hurried back from Muskoka where he had just started his holiday, and the Governor General, H.R.H. the Duke of Connaught, on vacation at Banff in the Rocky Mountains, started the four-day trip back to Ottawa, arriving in the early morning of August 4.

In British Columbia the Premier, Sir Richard McBride, bought two submarines from a firm in Seattle, privately built and intended for the Chilean government. The federal government bought them three days later, at no extra cost, on advice from the British Admiralty, but the subs remained to guard the west coast for as long as it was thought to be in danger from the German navy. On the east coast there came reports from Sidney, Nova Scotia, that two German cruisers had been sighted off St. Pierre and Miquelon.

In Ottawa, lights burned late in the Militia Department where the energetic Minister of Milita and Defence, Colonel the Honourable

Sam Hughes, prepared to mobilize a militia force. Across the Ottawa River in Hull, Quebec, the newly organized 70th Regiment guaranteed a force of at least fifteen hundred men from the vicinity, and similar offers of recruits poured in from all over the country, to the elation of the patriotic Minister.

Sam Hughes was born at Darlington, Ontario, in 1852, the son of Protestant Irish-Scots parents. He joined the Militia when he was thirteen and served in the Fenian Raids of 1870. Later he taught school, became a journalist, served eight months with the British in the South African War as a transport and intelligence officer, was elected to the Canadian Parliament in 1904 and entered the cabinet when the Conservatives came to power in 1911. He had been an outstanding athlete, a rifle shot of note, was a total abstainer from alcohol and tobacco, a rabid Orangeman and an ardent Imperialist. Unfortunately he had many strong prejudices and was as fanatical in his hatred of enemies as in his loyalty to friends.

Evidence of eccentric tendencies showed in a letter he wrote Prime Minister Sir Wilfrid Laurier in 1908 demanding a Victoria Cross for his services in South Africa. Three years later he wrote the recently installed Governor General, H.R.H. the Duke of Connaught, making the same demand, describing his leadership of British forces in gallant actions and the dismay of his commander, General Warren, "sobbing like a child" when Hughes decided to return to Canada.

This unusual behaviour increased with the years, but the new Minister attacked his job with enthusiasm and vigour, establishing an extensive cadet movement, building armouries, encouraging and supporting the Militia. He was devoted to Canada, and in the years before 1914, was convinced that war with Germany was inevitable. He bent every effort to prepare for it.

From east to west, Canada was divided into military districts or areas commanded by regular senior officers. Mobilization plans, based on a survey made by British Generals Sir John French and Ian Hamilton, called for such commanding officers to raise the required units within their own jurisdiction.

By 1914 Canada had a paper strength of 75,000 militiamen, but the regular army had barely 3,000 bodies, all ranks, for Hughes had a strong prejudice against regular soldiers which extended to Roman Catholics and French Canadians. Consequently he laid down policies with regard to appointments and recruiting that angered and humiliated many, particularly in Quebec, where unfortunate repercussions affected the future of the whole country.

On cabinet authorization of an expeditionary force of one division, the Minister ignored normal channels of command. He had telegrams sent direct to all commanders of militia units ordering them to enlist all volunteers. He then executed the truly extraordinary feat of building an assembly area, complete with watermains, electricity, railway sidings, target ranges and administrative buildings, all within the phenomenally short space of a few weeks. This was Valcartier Camp on the Jacques Cartier River, sixteen miles from Quebec City. In three weeks 35,000 men poured into the camp and went under canvas.

Colonel Hughes' original intentions had been to exclude all units of the Permanent Force, but two batteries of the Royal Canadian Horse Artillery and two cavalry regiments, the Royal Canadian Dragoons and Lord Strathcona's Horse, were mobilized in September and included in the contingent. The only regular infantry, the Royal Canadian Regiment, was dismayed at being sent to Bermuda for guard duty—relieving a British regiment.

Although there were already 226 militia regiments on which to draw, Colonel Hughes gave authority for an additional unit, raised and substantially financed by another veteran of the South African War, Captain Hamilton Gault of Montreal. It was named Princess Patricia's Canadian Light Infantry, for the Governor General's only daughter, and was unique in that its personnel consisted of nearly 90 per cent veterans from the British Isles and represented nearly every regiment and branch of the British forces, including artillery, marines, and Royal Navy. Seven days after enlistment opened the regiment had its full complement of men, commanded by Lieutenant-Colonel F. D. Farquhar, D.S.O., an experienced soldier then serving as Military Secretary to His Excellency, the Governor General.

Within a few days Canada had undertaken to send one division of 24,000 men to the aid of Britain, but in the first flush of enthusiasm, so many men enlisted so fast that there was little time to set up administrative organization, let alone train them.

In addition, the problem of clothing and equipping thousands of men was monumental, and there was little good about that which was chosen. An infantryman's accoutrements were carried on his back attached to a shoulder-harness with straps and belt. They consisted of a bayonet, entrenching tool, ammunition pouch, haversack and a pack with greatcoat and blanket.

The British army issued the Princess Patricias with equipment made of webbing which was light and easily adjusted to fit comfortably. Other infantry units suffered under the Canadian-made Oliver—a heavy pack with stiff leather harness and huge brass buckles that dug into the shoulders. It had a leather yoke in front which rode up under the chin and choked the wearer as weight dragged the pack down. Marching Canadian troops developed a distinctive convulsive heave of the shoulders to prevent strangulation.

The Ross rifle could not have been worse for active service. It was a fine precision-made sporting rifle, and as such Colonel Hughes knew it to be extremely accurate at long range. But its length made it unsuitable for the cavalry; the artillery found it slipped in the limber brackets and fouled the wheels; and as a weapon it failed the infantry when it was most needed. The gun required special care and special ammunition that was unavailable overseas. A few rounds of rapid fire caused it to heat and jam, and the heel of a heavy boot or an entrenching tool was needed to release the bolt, when seconds meant the difference between life and death. Canadians in battle soon learned to salvage British Lee-Enfields from the dead, but since they had to account for the Ross at inspection, many carried two rifles.

The issue of army boots was one more cross to bear. Neat and dressy, they were agony to march in and quickly rotted in the mud and water. There was more bitterness than humour in the troops' nickname for the Minister—Sham Shoes.

Later another curious piece of equipment was the MacAdam Shovel, named for its inventor, a lady secretary of Hughes'. It was made of heavy steel with a four-inch handle and a blade roughly eight by four inches. There were two loop-holes in the blade, a large one to shoot through, a smaller one for sighting. The idea was a combined entrenching tool and shield, but experience showed it to be ineffective as protection, awkward to dig with, and too heavy to carry. Hughes tried to press its adoption, terming tools of War Office pattern "absolutely useless for any purpose," but finally all were withdrawn and the MacAdams, purchased in Philadelphia for $36,000, were sold as scrap metal for $1,400. But these deficiencies were yet to be discovered.

The Camp Commandant at Valcartier was Colonel Victor A. S. Williams, the Adjutant General who was later sent to England in temporary command of the First Contingent. This was a surprising choice of the Minister's, for the Adjutant General—a senior staff officer at Army Headquarters—is a busy man, usually chained by administrative duties to his desk in Ottawa. Other senior commands were allotted: Lieutenant-Colonel M. S. Mercer, a Toronto businessman and a keen militiaman who had attended British army manoeuvres before the war, now headed the 1st Infantry Brigade; Lieutenant-Colonel A. W. Currie, an experienced militiaman who had held every rank from private to commanding officer, first of an artillery regiment, then a Highland battalion, was given the 2nd Infantry Brigade; Colonel R. E. W. Turner, V.C., D.S.O., a distinguished veteran of the South African War, took command of the 3rd Infantry Brigade. All were promoted to brigadier general. In addition there were many other experienced officers, South African veterans and members of the Northwest Mounted Police.

As Valcartier now bulged with over 32,000 untrained volunteers, the immediate urge was to get them overseas, and it was decided to ship them all to England for the British to sort out and train.

The First Contingent, therefore, was considerably larger than anticipated, and the unfortunate Director of Embarkation, Lieutenant-Colonel William Price, recently appointed but given no staff to work with, was responsible for its embarkation. The operation was bizarre; surely nothing like it has occurred before or since.

The task would have been simpler had the citizen soldiers obeyed orders and done as they were told, but discipline had yet to be learned. Most of them were British-born, returning to defend king and country, but among them were many rolling stones, soldiers of fortune, young men in whom the spirit of adventure burned brightly. A happy reckless breed, all were willing and eager to fight, but determined to wrest every ounce of fun from the adventure.

Embarkation was further complicated by the unpredicted need to find ships and space for seven thousand additional bodies with baggage, horses, wagons—all the paraphernalia of war. Pandemonium reigned while they loaded too many on ships too small, unloaded and tried again. Units were separated from their baggage and mounted units separated from their mounts. Too few grooms found themselves caring for too many horses, in some cases as many as sixteen apiece.

The 16th Battalion claimed "that their horses were put on board one ship, the harness on another, the wagons on another and the wheels on another." One ship set sail with the officers and men, bearing no relation to one another, who had missed the ships they should have been on, while in the hold was a miscellaneous collection of baggage belonging to heaven-knew-whom, that had been left on the docks. Finally, after the ships were loaded and out in the river, ammunition had to be ferried out to them, to comply with a belated order requiring so many rounds per ship.

The crossing was uneventful and the men passed spare time away indulging in a little good fun, not to be confused with recreational training. They climbed the rigging, fell overboard, and were rescued. An infantry regiment investigated one of the holds, found cavalry equipment for cavalry not aboard, and disembarked smartly spurred. Regular British army officers accompanying them were aghast at the shenanigans, but mid-October saw all in England, safe and fairly sound.

Because of submarine threats the convoy was diverted from Southampton to Plymouth, where facilities were limited. Captain J. F. C. Fuller (later Major-General of Tank fame) was then Deputy Assistant Director of Railway Transport. It was three weeks before the whole convoy was unloaded, but the first few days were a new experience for Captain Fuller. He describes the arrival of the Canadian Contingent in his book *Memoirs of an Unconventional Soldier*.

It was Fuller's job to get the Canadians and their baggage aboard trains for Salisbury Plain. This entailed the men marching through the town to the railway station. The baggage, piled mountain-high on the docks, had to be transported to the station by every vehicle he could commandeer. There was no attempt to sort it, just load and send it on its way, but the Canadians refused to handle it. "They had come to fight, not to do coolie work." This was no time to argue with untrained and as yet undisciplined troops, and Captain Fuller rounded up men from Kitchener's Army to do the job.

The baggage, the whole jumbled mass of it, eventually reached Salisbury Plain, where weeks were spent sorting it. The Canadians got there too—a few of them that same evening—but many who disembarked that first day cheerfully went absent without leave and failed to turn up for several days. Captain Fuller describes the scene.

The men were, for the most part, absolutely raw; they were met by rejoicing crowds and assaulted by every young and old harlot in the dual city. Men fell out or were pulled out of the ranks to vanish down side streets. A few reached the railway station, but the remainder painted Devonport and Plymouth pink, red and purple.

Next day the public houses were closed early, but by then the town was "swarming with drunks." Requisitioning a disused building, Captain Fuller turned it into a prison in which drunken Canadians were locked for twenty-four hours. A train labelled *Drunkard's Special* left each morning for Salisbury till all were disposed of.

Thus the First Canadian Contingent came to England. On October 14, Colonel Williams handed his command over to Lieutenant-General E. A. H. Alderson, a British officer, whose task it now was to whip the Canadians into fighting trim.

For a week or more, fine weather attended the pitching of tents and sorting of baggage. Then the rains came. For endless days and nights the heavens wept relentlessly, temperatures dropped, and gales flattened tents. Time and again men woke in the night to find themselves wrapped in soaking canvas.

In four months it rained 89 days, dumping 24 inches of water on the Plain and making of it a sea of mud. The chalk base prevented drainage and training was almost impossible. Illness was prevalent with some cases of the dread meningitis, and men longed to be sent to the battlefront—anything was better than wallowing on Salisbury Plain. The fallacy of that hope was soon to be discovered. Meanwhile they sloshed around the Plain learning to be soldiers.

Canadian Militia regulations of twenty years' standing required all militia canteens to be "dry." This was before Hughes' time, but he confirmed prohibition in the new army, and troops in Canada route-marched, singing to the tune of John Peel:

D'ye ken Sam Hughes
He's the foe of booze
He's the one champeen
Of a dry canteen.
Oh we'll all go to bed
For the camp is dead
And we won't have a head
In the morn————ing!

When similar restrictions were imposed in England the results were disastrous. Neighbouring towns and villages were by no means dry, and the troops seized every chance to leave camp and drink as much as they could as fast as they could. General Alderson and the Minister of Militia, now promoted major-general, never did get on, and one of their first bitter controversies was the dry versus the wet canteen. Alderson won. Wet canteens, serving beer only, were installed, supervised and controlled. The situation improved, although the ill-informed at home shook their heads, deploring the army's vending liquor to wholesome Canadian boys.

As training progressed considerable weeding-out had to be done, since the lack of discrimination in recruiting had resulted in men unfit or unsuitable for service. These were returned to Canada. The rest, with a zeal and enthusiasm that amazed regular soldiers, carried out in wet clothing—impossible to dry overnight—route marches, entrenching, foot and arms drill. Challenged by the known excellence in rifle fire of the British regulars, the Canadians, although hampered by limited ammunition and range facilities, developed a reputation for their countrymen as "natural shots," but their Ross rifles were already beginning to give trouble.

Besides war training, artisans within the contingent were called upon to build huts for the men and, more important, horse standings for the cavalry and artillery. The horses, hock-high in mud, with grooming well-nigh impossible, suffered grievously and their condition deteriorated until shelter was provided.

Artillery ranges were totally inadequate. Royal Canadian Horse Artillery batteries managed only one week of range practice because they shared facilities with six British divisions. Engineers, however, had more than adequate training, supplementing their military techniques with necessary construction and repairs on the camp.

Australian and New Zealand authorities took one look at the plight of the Canadians and diverted their troops, en route to England for training, to training grounds in Egypt. But the First Contingent showed their mettle that first winter on Salisbury Plain.

Everything was against them: confusion resulting from unorganized mass recruiting and subsequent embarkation; the sorting out in England; the training of raw recruits in appalling conditions with inadequate facilities. Incredibly, enthusiasm was maintained, morale high, all eager to get to France and into the fight before it was over.

British officers loaned by the War Office worked along with the new force, infected by their enthusiasm, giving guidance, counsel and encouragement. Some of them later commanded Canadian formations and served on the staff. There was also a good sprinkling of

Imperial officers who had been serving in Canada at the outbreak of the war. One of these, Major L. J. Lipsett, had been with the Permanent Force at Esquimalt, British Columbia, where he instructed and advised among others, the militiaman Arthur Currie. Lipsett, now a Lieutenant-Colonel, was the commanding officer of the 8th Battalion—Winnipeg's Little Black Devils—in Currie's 2nd Brigade.

In the following four years many British officers served with the Canadians and most of them did well, considering their time spent with the Corps as the happiest and most rewarding of their active service. The few who failed to adjust did not last long. By mutual consent their stay was brief.

That winter the Canadian Cavalry Brigade was formed. It was made up of the Royal Canadian Horse Artillery, the Royal Canadian Dragoons, Lord Strathcona's Horse and the 2nd King Edward's Horse, the last a British Special Reserve regiment that had been training units in Canada just prior to the war. The Fort Garry Horse, a militia regiment from Winnipeg, for the time being, became a reserve cavalry regiment, but soon replaced the British unit. The Brigade was put under the command of a British officer, Brigadier General J. E. B. Seely, although the Canadian government would have preferred a Canadian commander.

By February the 1st Canadian Division was judged ready for active service. His Majesty George V inspected it on the 4th; then leaving behind a disconsolate 4th Brigade and the 6th Fort Garry Horse as reserves, the "lucky" ones left for France.

2

THE 1st CANADIAN AUTOMOBILE MACHINE GUN BRIGADE

Princess Patricia's Canadian Light Infantry was not the only new unit to materialize that September. Another, a uniquely different formation, was the brain-child of a Frenchman of diverse talents.

Although Raymond Brutinel was an active figure in the Canadian West for nearly a decade before the war, his name is almost unknown to Canadians. He was born in 1882 in the province of Aude, France, in a village dominated by Mount Bonnet in the Pyrenees. His family dates back to the early seventeenth century, the Brutinels being mountaineers, sailors, soldiers and land people, proud of a blood-strain of Highland Scots. Being Huguenots, there was a long history of conflict with the government extending even into the twentieth century.

Brutinel emigrated to Edmonton, Alberta, in 1905 when he was twenty-three, bought a hundred acres of land and built a modern brick home on the south side of the St. Albert River. He joined a syndicate headed by E. B. Greenshields, a financier and director of the Grand Trunk Pacific Railway, and explored and prospected for mineral rights and water power as far as the headwaters of the Peace, Skeena, Pembina and McLeod rivers. He also forecast the discovery of oil near Edmonton.

When Alberta became a province, one of the questions in the political battle concerned religious and separate school rights for the French Canadians. The Liberals, who subsequently won, supported the French Canadians, and Brutinel, who knew what it meant to be deprived of religious rights, took charge of the politically Liberal French newspaper, *Le Courrier de l'Ouest,* owned by Philippe Roy, a Quebec-born senator who was later appointed to France as Commissioner General for Canada.

But Brutinel was not politically inclined. He was still a captain in the French army reserve, maintained a keen interest in military matters, and was a confirmed believer in the potential power of the machine-gun, a weapon for which most military men had nothing but contempt. Brutinel believed that properly employed, it could be the queen of a battlefield.

The history of the machine-gun is old, but the first "modern" version was invented by an American, Dr. Richard Gatling, about the time of the American Civil War, and saw service in several armies. Later the French developed the Mitrailleuse, a machine-gun invented by a Belgian. It was a secret weapon with which they hoped to win the Franco-Prussian War of 1870. Used properly to augment infantry fire-power, it would have been effective, but the French used it like artillery, mounted on a wheeled carriage, where it was a failure. The Vickers-Maxim was invented by another American in 1885 and was developed and modified by a British engineer, Albert Vickers. It turned out to be the best of its kind, but indifference on the part of the British War Office forced Vickers into selling a licence to manufacture to the German armament firm of Krupp.

The British had a small quantity of Vickers guns in the Boer War of 1899-1902, but made the same mistake as the French, until some radical thinker mounted them on tripods, where they proved their value.

But prejudice ran deep, and neither the French nor British had much use for the machine-gun despite its performance in the Russo-Japanese war in 1905. There observers from major countries saw the Japanese use it to mow down the hordes of Russian soldiers with devastating effect, but only the Germans grasped its significance. They returned to Germany to introduce solid machine-gun units into their military machine.

By 1914 Raymond Brutinel was a millionaire and living in Montreal. Even before war was actually declared he had received permission from the French Ambassador in Washington to take, at his own expense, a number of machine-guns to France and there rejoin the French army. Vickers guns were not available, but Brutinel was content to take what he could get—the Colt—and had negotiated with the Colt Company in Hartford, Connecticut, to supply the weapons.

But French cartridges, needed to adapt the guns to French ammunition, were not available in Canada or the United States, and by August 4, when Canada too was at war, the threat of German cruisers in the St. Lawerence closed the Port of Montreal.

Meanwhile Clifford Sifton, a prominent and wealthy lawyer who was later knighted, heard of Brutinel's scheme. Sifton had been a minister in the Liberal cabinet, and since his age precluded active service, he was anxious to help in other ways. He called on Brutinel, suggesting the plan be diverted to the Canadian army now mobilizing.

Brutinel was not long in seeing in this proposal an opportunity to introduce a radically modern innovation. Fire-power and mobility were recognized as primary essentials in war, but armies still moved by the muscular power of man and beast. In this age, why not *mechanical* power? In a new army not yet addicted to orthodoxy, this had exciting possibilities.

The two men discussed the idea, Sifton's quick mind grasping the fundamentals. He would put the proposition up to the Minister of Militia.

"First I must talk with my ambassador," Brutinel warned.

"Then let's call him on the phone right now," Sifton replied.

M. Juisserent, in Washington, approved.

"Canada and France are in the same boat," Brutinel remembers him saying. "Whatever you do for the one will accrue to the benefit of both. Join the Canadian Militia and God bless you!"

The two men got no sleep that night. Brutinel prepared notes on the fire-power and employment of machine-guns, the need for mobility, and the possibility of modifying commercial vehicles for the purpose.

Sifton took the notes to Ottawa and presented them to the Minister of Militia, together with the promise that the unit would be created out of private funds. Colonel Hughes received the proposal with enthusiasm, gave his approval and disclosed it to the press where it received wide circulation.

The list of contributors was never made public, but in addition to Brutinel and Sifton, who both subscribed substantially, other Canadians made handsome contributions. Believed to be among them were Vincent Meredith, (created a baronet in 1916) president of the Bank of Montreal; J. W. McConnell, publisher and financier; J. R. Booth, lumber magnate of Ottawa; and Herbert Holt, (knighted in 1915), a financier and president of the Royal Bank of Canada.

No time was lost. Major John Sifton, a son, undertook the many details of administration and set up headquarters in a suite of rooms in the Chateau Laurier Hotel in Ottawa. Brutinel left immediately for Hartford, Connecticut, to place an order for twenty Colt machine-guns; then to Ardmore, Pennsylvania, for vehicles made by the Auto Car Company, rugged delivery vans that had a reputation for reliability. The Bethlehem Steel Company provided armoured plate and Brutinel himself directed the design of the steel-protected bodies. He received generous co-operation from all three companies and in three weeks the consignments were ready.

At the Colt factory German workers guessed the destination of the guns from the calibre of the ammunition, and did all they could in the way of obstruction. The Colt manager arranged to smuggle the guns out of the plant ahead of schedule, and Brutinel picked them up in one of the armoured trucks and drove to Canada. Not far from the plant he ran into an ambush presumably laid by German sympathizers. Several shots were fired but the bullets bounced off the steel plates and did no harm.

The equipment arrived intact in Ottawa just one month from the time the unit was first conceived. An Order-in-Council authorized the formation of the 1st Canadian Automobile Machine Gun Brigade and recruiting opened on September 9. The suite in the Chateau Laurier served as a recruiting centre, but the crowds soon overflowed into the mezzanine as men answering an advertisement for recruits flocked to enlist, perhaps as much out of curiosity as anything else.

The Brigade comprised two batteries, the 1st and 2nd Sifton Batteries. The establishment called for ten officers headed by a major (Brutinel) and 124 other ranks. Twenty machine-guns, eight armoured motor cars, eight trucks and four automobiles completed the outfit. Of the overall personnel, 20 per cent were ex-soldiers, 5 per cent Canadian militiamen and the rest had no military training at all, being mostly chauffeurs and motor mechanics with a sprinkling of university students.

With no time for even basic training, it was a bedraggled outfit that H.R.H. the Duke of Connaught inspected on September 29 before it sailed with the First Contingent for England. Nevertheless it caught the Duke's imagination, and he wrote later to Major Brutinel expressing his interest in the unit and appreciation for the "generosity of the public-spirited gentlemen who had provided the funds."

The unit also caught the fancy of Canadians, for within the year three more machine-gun batteries were created through private subscription and later came under (by then) Colonel Brutinel's command. They were named the Eaton, Borden, and Yukon Batteries, named respectively after a generous donor, John Eaton, the Prime Minister, and the locale of the third's origin.

This last was raised by Joe Boyle, the Yukon millionaire whose adventurous career started long before he went to the Klondike. Kim Beattie has written a biography of this man, almost unknown today, but one of the most colourful Canadians in history.

He was born in Woodstock, Ontario. By the time he went to the North, he had packed a lifetime of adventure into his thirty years—as a boy, sailing before the mast in the Near and Far East, then financier, gambler and fight promoter in New York. He took the Australian heavyweight, Frank Slavin to the Yukon in 1897, but the fighter hated it and pulled out. Boyle stayed and became fabulously wealthy.

At his own expense Boyle recruited, equipped and brought to Ottawa the Boyle Mounted Machine Gun Detachment and presented it to the Canadian government with himself as commanding officer. The cap badge was a gold-pan atop crossed machine-guns with the initials Y.T. The original collar badge was said to be a gold-pan with a genuine nugget in the centre, which may explain why few if any exist today.

Sam Hughes accepted the detachment and rejected the commander, rewarding him with an honorary lieutenant-colonelcy and changing the name to the Yukon Battery. Whereupon Boyle, who was determined to get into the fight in some capacity, fought his own private war with Hughes, then stormed over to England and badgered Lord Kitchener.

To get rid of him, the War Office sent him to Russia as a member of the British Railway Mission, where he got things done—done well and quickly. When the revolution took place, Boyle got the Allied Missions out safely, then had incredible adventures in Russia, then in Romania. There, as adviser to the Romanian government, he tried to bring order out of chaos after the German conquest of 1917, and became a close personal friend of Queen Marie and her family. In 1919 he went to London where he raised a British force to fight the invading Hungarian Bolsheviks under Bela Kun, but political unrest continued to beset the Balkan States, and Boyle, who had given his health and fortune to Romania's cause, returned a few years later to London, there to die in poverty and alone.

Meanwhile the 1st Canadian Automobile Machine Gun Brigade, as yet only two batteries strong, arrived in England, settled down on Salisbury Plain, and in spite of miserable conditions, plunged enthusiastically into training. Their tongue-stumbling name was soon changed to the 1st Canadian Motor Machine Gun Brigade, and before long that was familiarly shortened to the 1st Motors, or just Motors.

Three out of four of the men had had no military training. There was a larger percentage with some mechanical knowledge, but few if any had ever handled a machine-gun, and they had no handbooks on the subject. These were a must, so while the personnel received basic military training, Major Brutinel, among other things, wrote a handbook on how to take a machine-gun apart, clean, repair and mount it. Machine-gunners learned to do this blindfolded, so that even under the most adverse conditions they could maintain guns in action.

All ranks had to master the whole procedure and at the start many quailed at the sight of a Colt gun, reduced to a mass of ill-assorted bits and pieces that must be put together. It took hours of labour and practice to re-assemble rapidly, but when they finally mastered this, the men of the 1st Motors then taught the machine-gunners of infantry battalions, whose quota of guns (previously two, as in the British army) had been raised to four.

Lack of firing ranges on the Plain prevented fire-practice and experience in the correction of stoppages, of which the Colt had a great many. Determined efforts to obtain temporary ranges were in vain. The preservation of grass sod was considered more important than training for a war that was already in progress, and exacting a heavy toll in men, equipment and prestige. It was almost impossible to fire any belts, and machine-gunners with the 1st Canadian Division, which left England in February, gained their experience murderously and wastefully on the battlefield.

The Motors were more fortunate. Although kept in England until June they were moved to coastal defence in Kent after the Division left, and there contrived to get target practice in limestone quarries.

There is some mysterious component in the process of promotion, by no means confined to the British, that seems to turn the brain of a promising young officer into bone by the time he assumes high command. Time and again it happens, and in spite of the known performance of machine-gunnery in previous wars, the British High Command refused to consider the weapon's potential. In the ten years immediately preceding the First World War, the War Office had ordered an aggregate of exactly one hundred and ten machine-guns—an average of eleven per year.

At Mons in August 1914, the volume of British rifle-fire had been so withering and so destructive that the enemy had mistaken it for a preponderance of machine-gun fire. The British were justly proud of the bravery and excellence of their professional, precision-trained riflemen, without recognizing the significance. One machine-gun manned by a crew of six could fire three hundred rounds of controlled aim in one minute. In the same time fifteen rounds was the best that a highly trained rifleman could maintain, and with the factors of human vulnerability, scattered fire was inevitable. What was more—most of the precision-trained riflemen were dead—their bodies rotting in the fields of Flanders. To the closed mind, seeing is not necessarily believing, but in August, September and October of 1914, the War Office in a panic move did place four separate orders with Vickers for a total of less than two thousand machine-guns.

Many comparatively junior officers in the British army had pressed for more machine-guns. One of these, Brigadier General Baker-Carr, was a strong advocate of "substituting machinery for brawn" as he called it, but was told tersely to mind his own business. Shortly after war started, he made it his business to set up a machine-gun training school behind the lines which was studiously ignored by General Headquarters Staff. But commanders in the fighting line showed themselves eager for whatever would give them more fire-power in relation to available men.

Brutinel was to meet this attitude many times in the next four years. He was most anxious to get Vickers machine-guns—which he considered "that machine-gun par excellence"—not only for the

Motors but for the whole Canadian contingent. He visited the Vickers plant and saw no evidence of full-time production, but no guns for the Canadians were available.

It was not until 1915, when the clamour from the front line could no longer be ignored, that David Lloyd George became Minister of Munitions and this situation was changed, and changed quickly, but not in time to help the 1st Division in their heroic battles in France that spring. Fortified German positions bristling with machine-guns took terrible toll. Against them the four-gun section of an infantry battalion, outnumbered but never out-classed, rapidly learned to handle their inferior guns.

Any illusions Brutinel might have had that the Higher Command was learning were dashed on February 4, 1915, when King George V inspected the Canadians, prior to the 1st Division's departure for France.

There was no place for such a radical unit as the 1st C.M.M.G.B. in a formal parade. However, Major Brutinel formed them up on three lines: the armoured cars and the officers' cars; the ammunition trucks and repair shops; and the auxiliary vehicles. In front of each armoured car stood the officer in command, the two Number One machine-gunners, and the driver. The rest of the crew crouched out of sight in the armoured car, on parade but invisible.

The King found the formation intriguing. He dismounted and went over to the first armoured car, ran his hand over the plate and walked around the vehicle. Suddenly, without warning, he put his foot on one of the wheels and hauled himself up to look inside.

Simultaneously, the men, hearing someone climbing up, rose, and eyeball to eyeball, over the side of the truck the King and the Canadians stared at one another.

The surprise was mutual, and the King nearly fell from his perch. The soldiers snapped to attention and the King burst out laughing, to the relief of all the King's men gathered round. Climbing down, he insisted on inspecting the whole unit, questioning closely about equipment, personnel and performance. He complimented Major Brutinel on his unit, and while waiting for his charger to be brought, turned to Lord Kitchener.

"This is a pretty useful unit," he said enthusiastically.

Kitchener shook his head.

"I'm afraid not, Your Majesty. It would be most difficult to employ, and throw out of balance the fire-power of a division."

Brutinel, close by, heard this with dismay. Outrage swelled in his breast and he longed to challenge the statement, but could only stand woodenly by. Later that day when the royal party had left, Lieutenant-General Alderson, commander of the Division, said to him:

"I believe Kitchener is right, Brutinel."

In vain Brutinel protested and argued; the word had been spoken. To him the stubborn resistance to constructive modern ideas was incredible. Incredible, too, to a civilian who was shortly to become Minister of Munitions. Lloyd George pressed for the formation of a special machine-gun corps, which received Royal Assent. Although authorized, it met with what seemed to the Minister deliberate obstruction. In his memoirs, he relates: "My capacity for amazement at professional repugnance to new ideas or new formations, had reached saturation point."

Despite mild disapproval and indifference on the part of the War Office, the Motors kept doggedly training. Brutinel says: "I think the reason they didn't oppose the Brigade was because they didn't know or understand the scheme. On general grounds, they were just opposed to machine-guns. It sounds rather strange, but these are the facts."

For the first six months Brutinel's position in the Canadian army had been precarious. The French War Office repeatedly requested his return to France, to take up his commission in the French army. However, when the Canadian government protested his removal vehemently, the War Office prevailed on the French to grant him authorization to stay with the Canadians to the end of the war. M. Poincaré, President of France, signed a decree to that effect and M. Briand, Minister of Justice, countersigned it. The advantages turned out to be twofold. Through Brutinel a close liaison was established between senior commanders of the Canadians and the French forces, engendering both confidence and understanding. More immediately, the commander of the 1st Motors was now assured of getting on with the job of training without interruption or disruption.

This was all in accord with Brutinel's own wishes, for he knew only too well the conservative die-hard thinking patterns of established armies. With the Canadians, he had fresh ground and a fairly free hand to work out his theories.

As it turned out, it was not the stubbornness or conservatism of military minds that partially thwarted his scheme. Fire-power combined with mobility had been the object of the Brigade from its inception. But after the first few weeks of warfare in Western Europe, the German advance had been halted, and the line stabilized behind trenches, earthwork and barbed-wire entanglements. At the end of six months the front was practically unchanged, and it was obvious that for the time being at least, there could be no mobile role for the Motors. It was a disappointment, but Brutinel envisaged the day when his unit would be used as originally intended, and he resisted repeated efforts of the Higher Command to take away his vehicles. He used them for transport, still maintaining the armoured trucks, all of which carried two machine-guns with 10,000 rounds of ammunition per gun, and a crew sufficient to man them. Over and over again they proved their usefulness in action, but the time was to come when they saved the day, plugging the breakthrough of the German army in March, 1918.

The Motors remained on coast guard duty all spring. Then in June, they too went to France, arriving during a period of inaction which permitted them to familiarize themselves with conditions.

3

1914-15: THE WESTERN FRONT AND THE SECOND BATTLE OF YPRES

The German invasion of Belgium which brought the British into the war started on August 4. The invaders expected protestations and possibly a token show of force from the Belgians. Instead, Albert, their king, marshalled his small army, inadequately trained and pitifully equipped, and made a heroic stand at the fortress city of Liège, which guarded the gateway to the Belgian plain. Once through this twelve-mile pass, marching troops would find a smooth and easy route to invade France.

To the surprise of the world the inexperienced little Belgian army resisted with courage and determination, holding up the German advance ten days. The Germans, enraged by this presumption, vented their fury on the people—soldiers and civilians alike—in brutal violence and butchery that formed the basis for future atrocity stories that were often exaggerated and unfounded.

Belgian resistance was crushed by the time the British two-corps army, 100,000 strong, under the command of Field Marshal Sir John French, landed in France in the middle of August. The first British-German engagement was the Battle of Mons on August 23. Lieutenant-General Sir Douglas Haig commanded the 1st Corps, Lieutenant-General Sir Horace Smith-Dorrien the 2nd; but it was on the latter that the full weight of the German blow fell. Considerably out-numbered, they held up the German advance twenty-four hours. The British claimed the battle as a victory, but it was the beginning of the historic, fighting "Retreat from Mons" on August 24, a withdrawal by the British and, to the south, by the French, that went on for days and nights.

Sir John French had considered making a stand at Le Cateau, but as the French were still retiring he changed his mind and issued orders to continue the withdrawal. But Smith-Dorrien's Corps was exhausted and depleted after the battle at Mons, and Haig's 1st Corps, which should have joined up on their left, was six miles to the east, leaving a serious gap. By the night of the 25th the 2nd Corps reached Le Cateau, having covered between twenty and thirty miles, fighting rearguard actions all the way. Many men were literally asleep on their feet; Sir Horace halted, and prepared, under direct orders from French, to resume the retreat next day.

His 4th Division was still out fighting a rearguard action when word came that the Germans were advancing rapidly. The Corps must move on at once or be prepared to fight at dawn. General H.Q. was twenty-six miles distant, and there was no direct contact to the Commander-in-Chief. Sir Horace had to make the decision. There was no other choice but to fight—the 4th Division could not be abandoned. His troops were almost unconscious with fatigue, sleeping where they stopped—in the rain, on cold cobblestones, with packs still on their backs. But a few hours' sleep would make new men of them.

Early next morning, battling in the streets of the town, men of what the Kaiser called "Britain's contemptible little army" caught the enemy by surprise. Greatly out-numbered, they inflicted 9,000 casualties and held the Germans at bay for six hours, suffering themselves better than 8,000 dead and wounded. Then, breaking off the battle, they resumed their orderly retreat.

These Britons, ill equipped for modern war, nevertheless constituted one of the best-trained, disciplined armies in the world. Thereafter, with typical British humour, the men proudly called themselves the Old Contemptibles, but such was the slaughter in the first year that few remained to tell of it.

The Allied retreat and the German advance continued till the line was dangerously near Paris. Then the Battle of the Marne took place at the end of the first week in September. Together the French and British defeated the Germans, who began falling back till the battle line extended from the North Sea, just west of Ostend, in a southerly direction through Soissons, Rheims and Verdun.

The British were soon reinforced to make First and Second Armies under the former Corps commanders and they moved north into Flanders where the month of October saw them engaged in a series of indecisive battles to be called the Battles of Ypres, 1914. Here a deadlock ensued. The Germans were now occupied with the Russians on the Eastern Front and Britain was feverishly turning civilians into soldiers and, not too successfully, stepping up the production of arms and ammunition. Neither side wanted to take the offensive; thus it became a war of attrition with both sides clinging tenaciously to their positions for wretched and monotonous weeks that stretched into months, then years, while the battle line remained almost unchanged.

In their extremity, men on both sides took to ditches for what protection they gave. Then, even while battles raged, they dug holes in the ground, scooping with bare hands when entrenching tools, at best in short supply, were lost or unavailable. Cavalrymen, with no use for their horses, hacked away at the ground with swords, thanking God for the all too few picks and shovels they could extort from native peasants.

Hopefully all believed it to be only temporary, but the ditches soon made a defensive line with breastworks of earth and sandbags in front and a similar wall behind—a parados—to protect men from bursting shells. To check enemy attack, coil upon coil of barbed wire was spread in the foreground. Depth of trenches depended on the time available to dig and the nature of the ground, and a sort of Greek-key pattern of bays and traverses was adopted instead of straight lines in case the enemy captured a section of the trench.

Gradually refinements were added—dugouts, communication and supply trenches, and rear and forward lines. The winters were almost intolerable, for rain and snow fell relentlessly on men exposed day and night, up to their knees in water in ever-sodden clothing. Flanders was the worst. There the rainy season starts in late summer and much of the ground is reclaimed from marshland. Soon the shelling and tunnelling destroyed the drainage; there was no run-off and over the years conditions worsened.

Sanitation, of course, was primitive. Lice soon fed on the bodies of the living, rats on the bodies of the dead. Clothing became impregnated with the slimy, foul-smelling mud, and the stench of death and latrines was so prevalent that only the newcomers noticed it.

Food in the trenches was always scarce; a day's ration was a tin of bully beef, hardtack, a billy-can of tea and possibly a sweet sticky mixture called plum and apple jam. The troops swore it was made of turnips and rhubarb.

This was the world to which Princess Patricia's Canadian Light Infantry, the first Canadian unit to see action in France, were introduced on Christmas Eve, 1914. They had sailed from Canada with the First Contingent, but were not part of the Canadian Division. They were attached to the British 27th Division, in the 5th Corps of the Second Army commanded by Sir Horace Smith-Dorrien. Since most of the Patricias were veterans, the fact that they had had little recent training was not serious. Fortunately for them they were relieved of their Ross rifles, given British Lee-Enfields, and their Colts were replaced with Vickers machine-guns. The British had not yet learned about machine-guns, and there were only two, or at best four to a battalion, to be used in defence.

After a short indoctrination into trench warfare, the Patricias in January 1915 relieved a French battalion near St. Eloi. The trenches were in appalling condition, like open drains, and water was over boot-tops, often knee high. Sometimes a mere thirty yards separated opposing forces, and such close quarters made the use of artillery by either side out of the question. The British were woefully short of the implements of war, particularly machine-guns and hand grenades, and the troops soon learned to make their own bombs—jam tins stuffed with explosives and fired by a fuse. Because of the name of the jam-maker, these bombs were known as "Tickler's Artillery." After a few disastrous errors in leaving too long a fuse, which gave the enemy time to throw them back, the Patricias, too, became adept at making and using them.

Britain, by her shortage of arms and ammunition, showed that she was unprepared for war; high-level planners persistently believed the war could only last a few months and so did little long-range planning for replacements of men and supplies.

It was the Patricias who first earned the Canadians their reputation as raiders. During February suspicious noises and activity indicated that the Germans were up to something close by. The Royal Flying Corps, then in its infancy, reported the enemy to be digging a tunnel towards the British line. This was too close for artillery to shell. Hand-to-hand combat with bayonet and bomb was the only effective way to deal with the situation. It was a job for the 27th Division, and the Patricias were chosen.

In the dead of night some twenty-five men carrying picks, shovels and bombs wriggled across the mud to the German lines and with guttural shouts, jumped into their trenches. Although vastly outnumbered, the Canadians surprised and demoralized the enemy, killing many. The pick-and-shovel men demolished the tunnelling and the raiders withdrew, successful but not without losses. As the war progressed, raids were to become a specialty of Canadians, calling as they did for individual courage and initiative, which they displayed in abundance.

Meanwhile the 1st Division landed in France at St. Nazaire and entrained for a five-hundred-mile roundabout journey to Hazebrouck and the front lines. There in a relatively quiet sector they had a practical initiation into trench warfare under the tutelage of British regulars.

Early in March the British First Army engaged in a disastrous action at Neuve Chapelle, and here the Canadian Division had their first taste of battle. Fortunately, their participation was light and their casualties at a minimum. After that they had a few days in rest billets.

There were various types of rest billets, from the shelter made of sandbags with a tarpaulin top, no floor and few comforts, to the really "cushy" still-inhabited village where the engineers might have built three-tiered bunks in dry barns. Chicken wire served as good springs in the bunks. In between these two extremes there might be a Nissen hut of corrugated steel with floor, doors, but no windows. Most common was an abandoned village where soldiers made do with what they could find. Field kitchens were always at hand and the men had regular meals. For breakfast there was tea and hardtack with jam and sometimes bacon; for dinner beef or mutton stew, fried fish, pork and beans or, very occasionally, roast beef. All were good, but sometimes rabbit stew appeared and that was universally loathed. Supper was the same as breakfast, but extra "pickings" might be scrounged around the countryside. In the few days of rest men washed and mended their clothes, smartened up with some drill, took part in sports and on one evening had a company "smoker" where beer was free and sing-songs rowdy.

The 1st Division enjoyed their brief rest, but they were eager to tangle with the enemy and prove their mettle. They returned to the front line to join Major-General Plumer's 5th Corps along with the Patricias, still part of the British 27th Division. The Army Commander, Lietenant-General Sir Horace Smith-Dorrien had commanded Canadians in the South African War and now he expressed his pleasure at having them with him again and welcomed them to the Second Army.

It was only a few weeks later in the latter part of April that the Division learned, during the second Battle of Ypres, what hell war is. There for the first time the Germans used gas. French colonial troops on the immediate left of the 3rd Canadian Brigade suffered the brunt of the horror.

The action took place in the Ypres Salient and the Division was on the left flank of the 5th Corps. Two Highland battalions (the 13th and 15th) and Winnipeg's 8th Battalion were on the extreme left, adjoining a French Colonial division of Algerians and Zouaves. Their 4,500-yard line straddled a valley in front of Gravenstafel Ridge and included St. Julien, a key-point to bridgeheads and communication. The first week the Canadians spent furiously repairing and rebuilding deplorably inadequate defences, while intermittent shelling by both sides went on.

April 22, 1915, bright and clear, seemed like other days until late in the afternoon. Then, without warning, a savage artillery barrage swept the African and Canadian sectors, destroying the work of days and reducing the trenches and earthworks to beyond their original dilapidation. As the bombardment lessened, the Canadians saw a greenish-yellow cloud creeping across no-man's-land, enveloping the trenches of the Africans as it made its inevitable way towards them. The French line disintegrated. Without warning or understanding, the Turcos, Zouaves—gasping, stumbling, strangling—clutched their throats and died, or fled in panic.

After the cloud came the Germans, sweeping through the gap left by the Colonials, past and around the Brigade's flank. The Highlanders, greatly out-numbered, stood firm. The concentration of gas had missed them, but the hand-to-hand combat was bloody. Many Canadians died where they stood.

British counter-attacks throughout the next forty-eight hours achieved no lasting success, but the Canadian front, shortening as necessity demanded, held fast. Then early in the morning of the 24th the Germans used gas again.

This time the full concentration caught a company of the 15th Battalion and one of the 8th. They suffered grievously, but neither gave way. They met the advancing enemy with rifle and bayonet. Aided by a British regiment, but without artillery support, the 15th slowed, but could not repel, the attack. Surrounded on three sides, subjected to systematic and deliberate annihilating shellfire, the remnants of one company surrendered.

The 8th Battalion fared better. Mounting the parapets, those who survived the gas fired point-blank at the attacking Germans, fighting their jamming Ross rifles as vigorously and blasphemously as they did the enemy. With support from their own field artillery they held the ground, but to the left was a wide gateway through which the enemy surged.

Communications were almost non-existent except for runners, and situations changed so rapidly that British GHQ was confused as to what was actually happening. Misinformation and contradictory orders added to the confusion. Units were ordered to attack distant positions already under attack from other units; orders failed to reach other battalions, and there was ambiguity as to the sites of selected rendezvous.

Meanwhile breakthrough succeeded breakthrough. Along the Canadian-British line units lost touch and were isolated. Artillery support was uneven and insufficient; reinforcements were slow in arriving, if at all, and in the following days of severe fighting positions were relinquished as the line fell back. But the 1st Canadian Division fought with a tenacity and bravery that astonished the professionals.

There is now ample evidence that German prisoners and deserters, as well as Allied intelligence, had warned the Higher Commands—British and French—of impending gas attacks. Even the date was given, but weather conditions forced several days' postponement. General Smith-Dorrien had urgently advocated that measures be taken to offset such an attack, but Sir John French sharply reprimanded him for spreading pessimistic and alarming rumours.

Smith-Dorrien had already shown superiority of generalship earlier when British G.H.Q. was fraught with indecision and over-caution. Now in the face of continuing massacre of British troops, he recommended withdrawal to the eastern face of the Salient to more easily defended positions further removed from the domination of enemy fire. But

French, whose many shortcomings included poor judgment of when to fight and when to retire, was shaken by the reverses, unsure of himself, jealous of Smith-Dorrien's able generalship. Among other derogatory allegations, the Commander-in-Chief said of the Second Army Commander: "His pessimism has the worst effect on his commanders and his troops." Shortly after he sent a message "in clear" so many could hear it, telling Sir Horace to hand over his command and staff to General Plumer. So departed one of the ablest generals on the Western Front.

This terrible battle inspired what became the best-known poem of the First World War. Barely behind the front lines a medical officer named John McCrae had his dressing station. Born in Guelph, Ontario, in 1872, McCrae studied medicine at McGill University, but volunteered for the South African War as a lieutenant in the Artillery. Returning to Canada, he became a physician of note and pathologist at the Royal Victoria Hospital in Montreal. When war broke out in 1914, Dr. McCrae, although a gunner at heart, joined the Medical Corps where he felt he could best contribute. He was a poet and a lover of man and beast.

The suffering at Ypres caused McCrae great anguish. Rifle-fire and shells burst all around his dressing station and he writes in a letter home: "Gas fumes blow down from the infantry trenches and some comes from shells; one's eyes smarted and breathing was very laboured."

His close friend, Major-General Sir E. W. B. Morrison, at that time commanding 1st Brigade, Canadian Field Artillery, tells of McCrae: "My headquarters were in a trench on the top of the bank of the Ypres Canal and John had his dressing station in a hole dug in the foot of the bank. During periods in the battle men who were shot actually rolled down into his dressing station."

Visiting his friend one day, the medical officer diffidently read a scribbled poem he had written. Morrison rescued it from the waste basket where McCrae tossed it, and sent it to *Punch* magazine. "In Flanders Fields" came out in the issue of December 1915. The original copy, along with a small sketch of Morrison's, illustrating the poem—a temporary Canadian cemetery with its rows of white crosses among a tangle of poppies—now form part of a Colonel John McCrae display in the Royal Regiment of Canadian Artillery Museum at Camp Shilo, Manitoba. In January 1918, after four years of exhaustive work, McCrae died of pneumonia in a Canadian hospital in Boulogne.

The 1st Division went out of the line on April 25 and 26. In that Second Battle of Ypres, Britons and Canadians fought shoulder to shoulder with outstanding bravery against tremendous odds, but during the first crucial days the main pressure had come down on the flank of the 1st Division. By their determined stand during those vital days, the Division gave time for reinforcing Allied troops to arrive and end the threat of a breakthrough. A War Office communiqué, referring to the first three days, stated: "The Canadians had many casualties but their gallantry and determination undoubtedly saved the situation."

4

FREZENBURG, FESTUBERT, GIVENCHY, AND THE CANADIAN ARMY CORPS

After suffering more than 6,000 casualtics, all ranks, the Division had a brief respite. But the P.P.C.L.I. were to remain in the area until May 21, and by then had lost nearly 700 officers and men. In almost six consecutive weeks in the line, the Patricias had already shown themselves equal to the 1st Division's stature, but their stand at Frezenberg Ridge on May 8 was epic.

Weeks earlier their commanding officer, Lieutenant-Colonel Farquhar, had been killed by a sniper's bullet. Captain Buller, in the absence of the wounded Major Hamilton Gault, took over command, but on May 4 Buller was wounded in the head, a shell splinter in his eye. Major Gault, just back on duty, assumed a command that was to last only a matter of days.

The regiment's losses were already high, and in view of diminishing numbers, Major Gault ordered every man in the battalion—batmen, grooms, signallers—forward into support trenches.

At dawn on the 8th they came under the heaviest bombardment yet experienced by any troops, and shortly afterward Major Gault was wounded for the second time. By nine a.m. all field and company officers were casualties, either wounded or dead. Command devolved on Hugh Niven, a young lieutenant who a few months before had been a private in the ranks. By this time the Battalion was completely cut off. The field telephone was smashed, no messenger could penetrate the intense fire, poisonous gas drifted over the battlefield, ammunition was low. Thus the Patricias waited for the bayonet charge that was bound to follow the bombardment.

When it came, the Pats' steady fire drove them back, time after time, hour after hour, making every bullet count. Two of their machine-guns, with crews, received direct hits from shells. The other two kept firing.

Eventually reinforced by the 4th Rifle Brigade, they were relieved shortly before midnight, their casualties by then 392 for the day's fighting. Four officers and 150 men were left.

Meanwhile the 1st Division had not long to catch its breath or lick its wounds. South of the Salient the First Army under Sir Douglas Haig attacked at Aubers Ridge on May 9, but in twelve hours' fighting they made no gains, and lost 11,000 men. The attack was not resumed.

But on May 15 they attacked again after sixty hours' preliminary barrage by artillery, this time shortening the front to the southern point of the Ridge at Festubert. The Canadians who were to take part were transferred from the Second Army to the First, coming under Haig's command. Their hated Ross rifles were now replaced by Lee-Enfields on explicit orders from the Commander-in-Chief, Sir John French.

Festubert was another disaster. As one Canadian put it later, getting out alive was one of the few pleasant recollections. They attacked over water-logged fields devoid of cover, subjected to heavy bombardment, and worst of all, the murderous hail of machine-gun bullets.

The 3rd Brigade was commanded by Brigadier General Turner. Their objective was the capture of a a small orchard—known later as Canadian Orchard—which was strongly defended. Every house or other building in the German sector was a machine-gun nest, reinforced with sandbags and concrete, and their irregular dispositions required individual assaults. That men could live through such defensive fire from the enemy seemed a miracle, but a few of the attackers did, took the orchard and consolidated their gain as much as German artillery would permit. One commanding officer remarked sadly: "It cost a lot, but they did it!"

The 2nd Brigade attack, under Brigadier General Currie, was not so successful. Their objective was a point on the map designated as K5, but maps of the day were grossly inaccurate, blown-up versions of local French maps, and a similarity of symbols for different features was confusing. In some cases they were printed upside down with the north at the bottom of the sheet. With errors up to 450 yards, it was not only easy to get lost, it was hard not to.

After a personal reconnaissance, Currie asked that the attack be postponed a day, but this was refused and, in addition, artillery support was reduced. At first they made a minor advance. Then the bombers, with their variety of grenades—among them the jam-tin, the "improved hairbrush" and the "un-improved hairbrush"—moved forward in advance of the attacking infantry. Emerging single file, without cover of any sort, into direct fire from enemy machine-guns, they were cut down without a chance. The company commander called a halt. For the time being, to continue was sheer murder.

Throughout the battle, which was to last five days, artillery support was ineffective. It was curtailed, not by the Higher Command, but by the munition factories which were still turning out war materiel in penny packets. A battalion's four Colt machine-guns, gallantly handled but mechanically inferior, were no match for the massed guns of the Germans. The eastern hedge of the orchard, gained by the 16th Battalion on the first day, remained in Allied hands until it fell to the enemy in the spring of 1918, but elsewhere the whole British attack proved inconclusive and woefully expensive.

Before the end, dismounted cavalry of Seely's Brigade arrived on the scene. The Royal Canadian Dragoons and Lord Strathcona's Horse volunteered as reinforcements. Leaving their horses in England, and with no experience whatever of trench warfare, they entered the front line. They fought hard, but against the superiority of German artillery and machine-guns they fared no better than those they supported.

Although by now reduced to two-thirds of its original strength, the Division had another brief respite. Their next ordeal took place at Givenchy where they relieved a battalion of Guards on June 7. By now the Canadians, as a fighting force, were learning a few things on their own.

Assaulting troops in the face of enemy machine-guns invited annihilation. Numerical superiority meant nothing—fire-power everything. Brigadier General Mercer's 1st Brigade bore the brunt of this action which began on June 15, and was more in the nature of a raid. Here, they had time for preparation and support from the Royal Canadian Horse Artillery under Lieutenant-Colonel H. A. Panet. It was hoped that Canadian 18-pounders would destroy the enemy's wire, but means had to be found to combat enemy machine-guns. This was to be attempted by fitting three 18-pounders with armour plate and dragging them forward with muffled wheels, first by horses, then man-handled to the front line and concealed by camouflage.

At zero hour long-prepared mines were blown in front of the German lines. The artillery pounded away at the barbed wire and the forward guns raked the German lines for invisible machine-gun nests. Disastrously, the mines that should have destroyed the German strong-points were far from successful. They also detonated Canadian bomb depots, destroyed part of the line, and inflicted casualties on Canadians themselves. The wire-cutting by the artillery advertised where the enemy could expect attack, and heavy fire was concentrated on the corridor of cut wire. When the forward Canadian guns started firing, they disclosed their position, immediately drew enemy fire, and were destroyed, save for one hidden in a farmhouse where the gunners withheld fire for fear of hitting their own men.

In spite of everything, the men of the 1st Brigade managed to occupy part of the German forward line, but after a hopeless three-hour battle, they were withdrawn. In the barrage of bombs and gas shells, their numbers were rapidly diminishing. The Germans were by then massing for an assault, and the Canadians stood in the line of British artillery fire.

Givenchy was another reverse. Nevertheless, participation of the 1st Brigade had added to Canada's lustre. More important, Canadians were learning what the British were slow to grasp: that daylight raids without powerful and effective fire-power and preparation were worse than useless—they were grimly suicidal.

A few days later the 1st Canadian Division marched off for a well-earned rest.

It was just after this that the 1st Canadian Motor Machine Gun Brigade arrived in France to join the Division, and here Brutinel, now a Lieutenant-Colonel, started missionary work on the 1st Division commander, Lieutenant-General Alderson.

Alderson, who had helped dash Brutinel's hopes on the day of the King's inspection in February, now confessed that at the time he had no clear idea regarding the employment of the Machine Gun Brigade.

With battle experience behind him he had seen for himself the power of machines against men, and he told the Brutinel to familiarize himself with prevailing conditions, referring him to Brigadier General Seely, commander of the Canadian Cavalry Brigade, which, dismounted, had reinforced the Division at Givenchy.

For the next few months things were relatively tranquil for all the Canadians. They moved to a position slightly north of Armentières, a 4,400-yard front between Ploegsteert and Messines. They had time to rest and re-fit, digging in with second- and third-line trenches connected by communication trenches, through which ration parties, engineers, ammunition carriers and stretcher-bearers could pass back and forth in comparative safety. Snipers were active and patrols made forays, but there were only occasional clashes and shelling was not serious. Adapting to trench life was the worst thing the Canadians had to contend with. There were respites of course when men went out of the line to rest billets, but the misery and filth of trench life is fortunately beyond imagination and it was to be endured for three more years.

During the summer steps had been taken to organize the Canadian Expeditionary Force into an Army Corps. Corps troops were provided and with the arrival of a second division, General Alderson opened his Corps Headquarters on September 13. Major-General Currie succeeded Alderson as commander of the 1st Division and Major-General Turner took command of the 2nd. About this same time the Borden Machine Gun Battery arrived and joined the 1st Motors which now became Corps troops.

The Motors promptly busied themselves setting up machine-gun posts in strongly reinforced farm buildings. One such post was in the stable of the nearby Château La Hutte. The Château itself had been used by the Germans as a ranging mark and was now a ruin, but rubble made its cellar increasingly safe. A section billeted there could be relatively warm and cosy—men off duty passing the time playing poker. One of them—a lad of seventeen who later as Dr. Mark Marshall became a noted ophthamologist in Western Canada—was considered too young to gamble. Unperturbed by this paternal concern, he lost himself in reading whenever and whatever he could.

One night the sergeant said to him quietly: "That pile of bricks in the corner—where did they come from? The wall's secure. I can't account for them."

The youngster looked at the corner.

"That's right sergeant. Looks as though someone had lugged the stuff in."

"Keep mum about it. Tomorrow we'll take time out and investigate."

Next day the sergeant arranged for two more men to return early to the billet and they went to work on the rubble. It didn't take them long, and their search revealed a locked door. This gave no trouble. Behind it, a flight of stairs led to a sub-cellar and yet another door. Breaking this lock, they discovered the treasure—a great stock of excellent wine, each cobwebbed bottle labelled with the district and date of its vintage.

The rest of the section was let in on the secret and there was no shortage of volunteers that night when the sergeant ordered a deep pit dug in the garden and the bottles transported. Placed carefully in the pit, a few inches of earth over each layer, a cache of dozens of bottles was finally covered with earth, boards and rubble.

It was then the sergeant told the battery officer of the find. The captain was delighted.

"Good for you, sergeant. We'll stock the mess, but first take some for the men. There's lots here."

The sergeant accepted gratefully.

There was still a surplus when the mess had been stocked, so the divisional commander was offered a share. General Currie accepted a supply on behalf of the headquarters mess, but insisted on sharing it with the officers of the Motors, who refrained from mentioning that their own storeroom was strained to capacity.

With strong-points established and manned, the Motors formed mobile anti-aircraft sections and scouted up and down the road taking pot-shots at reconnoitring enemy aircraft. Canadians took pride in the fact that they had lost few guns, but the 14th Battalion unexpectedly recovered one they had never hoped to see again when machine-gun fire downed a German reconnaissance plane, just behind their lines. Men of the 14th tried to investigate the wreck but were driven back by enemy fire. When night fell, they crept out and collected maps, photographs, the first wireless sending-set to be discovered, and a Colt machine-gun that the battalion had lost months before at St. Julien.

Although the front was relatively quiet, the Canadians worked hard that autumn adjusting to their new formation. General Currie, concerned about the defence of his front, ordered Brutinel and a senior engineer officer to study the battle area, locating and organizing strong-points with a view to reducing the number of men in the front lines.

With this in mind, Brutinel conceived the idea of long-range, direct machine-gun fire that could be used to support the front line, and the further possibility of indirect fire, such as used by artillery. He prepared contour maps with trajectories of machine-gun fire, at various ranges, plotted on the same scale. Then a clay and plaster relief map was made of the area, including La Hutte Ridge down to Ploegsteert.

This study revealed that the Germans, from a position about 500 yards behind their own front line could, with indirect machine-gun fire, sweep the reverse slopes of La Hutte Ridge, where the Canadians were located. So far they had not employed indirect machine-gun fire, but Brutinel saw no reason to suppose they might not begin, since the range was too close for artillery. On the other hand, from positions well back of their own front lines, the Canadians could harass the front and support-lines of the Germans.

Brutinel hastily conveyed this information to General Currie, who saw the possibilities and ordered the idea tested. Five hundred yards behind the enemy lines German artillery officers could be seen, practically every day, congregating at the same hour. This was an ideal target.

With the guns in the stables of the Château La Hutte, about 2,000 yards from the proposed target and 1,500 yards behind their own lines, the Motors opened up, four guns at a time, with excellent effect. They scuppered the Germans several times before the latter retaliated by bringing up an 8-inch naval gun, firing ten rounds into the ruins of the Château. With the Canadian machine-gunners safe in the stable, and the wine safe in its hideout, there were no casualties, but the bombardment levelled the Château.

To Brutinel the possibilities were exciting. Why could not overhead fire be used as a protective barrage for infantry, supporting an advance or covering a withdrawal? This radical theory was immediately tested behind the lines on a small machine-gun range at Camiers. When convinced of its efficacy, the training of officers, N.C.O.'s and gunners began.

Having experienced the withering fire of enemy machine-guns in the spring, the Canadians fully appreciated the importance and destructiveness of the weapon, but it was a long time before Brutinel's theories were adopted throughout the Corps. Critics condemned them because human error in calculations could be disastrous, but soon a graph was developed that made reckoning quick, easy and practically foolproof. By the time the Corps participated in the Battles of the Somme a year later, Canadian machine-gunners were experts.

Meanwhile Brutinel organized brigade machine-gun companies with a strength of ten officers and 161 other ranks—three companies to a division (later increased to four to provide reserves and replacements). Worked out by Brutinel and Currie, it was endorsed by General Alderson, by now a convert.

At first there was an understandable lack of enthusiasm on the part of the infantry to the innovation of overhead fire. The training of crews entailed night firing—practically every night under all weather conditions. This made the infantry nervous and casualties were attributed to the machine-guns. Consequently every casualty thus reported was investigated and it was found that not a single case was due to the Canadian fire. Invariably they were proved to be inflicted by enfilade fire from German fixed rifles.

This was a great relief to all because a characteristic of the Colt gun, with which they were still equipped, was that the first bullet falls short. Close observation had to determine just how short, and this proved to be 200 yards from the firing point. When asked by a sceptic how he intended to overcome this fault, Brutinel replied: "We always remove the first round." But a more practical solution was to keep a margin of 500 yards ahead of the point of trajectory.

It was late September of that year that the British First Army engaged in the terrible battle of Loos, where the cream of Britain's youth flung themselves, in broad daylight, against uncut enemy wire. Thousands of young men were cut down by massed machine-gun fire—even the Germans were appalled at the useless assaults. An enemy diarist writes that when the wounded tried to crawl back to the British line "no shot was fired at them from the German trenches for the rest of the day, so great was the feeling of compassion and mercy for the enemy after such a victory."

As at Neuve Chapelle in the spring, the Canadians were again fortunate in playing only a minor role. The Royal Canadian Horse Artillery concentrated fire on roads and battery positions to prevent movement of German reinforcements, and the infantry made diversions by appearing to prepare for attack. They burned wet straw to simulate gas or smoke-screen and drew fire by dangling dummy figures over the trenches. This engaged the attention of opposing troops who otherwise might have been withdrawn to reinforce the German position.

Early in December an action occurred reminiscent of Givenchy but with happier results.

Where the Messines-Ploegsteert road passed through the Canadian line it was heavily protected with wire, barricades and machine-guns. The 1st Motors' batteries often cruised up the road at night to harass enemy communication trenches. A few hundred feet in front of this barrier, the Germans had erected a similar barricade, and one night a Canadian patrol discovered them digging and wiring a sap—that is, a trench running towards opposing lines with the object of establishing a forward listening post or machine-gun strong-point.

This had to be destroyed. The artillery tried unsuccessfully; a long line of trees protected it. Patrols, supported by machine-guns, tried bombing it but with no better luck. Then General Currie ordered a field gun brought forward. As soon as it was dark the barricade was breached sufficiently to manhandle the gun into a firing position in front.

The big gun fired twenty-six rounds at point-blank range and infantry followed up the assault. The position was destroyed and the few surviving Germans captured, at the cost of two Canadians slightly wounded. The gun was then withdrawn and the barrier replaced before daylight.

The Canadians were rapidly learning the art of war.

5

1916: THE BATTLE OF THE ST. ELOI CRATERS

Canadians enjoyed patrols—scouting in search of information, capturing prisoners if possible. The Germans patrolled too, but they were not as adept, and often got captured instead of capturing.

As no major operations fell to the Canadians in the winter of 1915-16, the Higher Command advocated a policy of "aggressive activity" to offset the demoralization of boredom and idleness. During the first winter the British had staged numerous successful raids, and in February 1915 the Patricias had made a name for themselves near St. Eloi. Now the Canadian Corps was encouraged to implement "natural Red Indian tendencies" and harass the enemy with raids.

Their first major venture was carried out in November on a position across the Douve River called La Petite Douve Farm. The 5th and 7th Battalions were singled out for the job; ten officers and 170 men withdrew behind the lines to rehearse night and day on ground as closely resembling the objective as possible. The farm was known to be heavily defended; seemingly shattered farm buildings had been reinforced and bristled with machine-guns.

The day before the raid enemy wire and the farm itself were heavily shelled. When night came the masked raiders crept forward to their respective areas, carrying portable bridging ladders and specially prepared mats for crossing wire. The men of the 5th Battalion got entangled in underwater wire, alerted the sentries and drew their fire. They were forced to withdraw, but without casualties. Those of the 7th Battalion reached their objective and took the enemy by surprise. They killed or wounded thirty or more Germans, captured a dozen prisoners and learned much useful information. The whole operation was so well carried out that the raiders returned with most of their special equipment; the only casualties were one killed and one slightly wounded.

From that time on, trench raids played a big part in Canadian operations. They became so successful and the raiders so expert that soldiers considered it a mark of honour to be chosen for a "war-party" and looked upon no-man's-land as strictly Canadian territory.

Types of raids varied as time progressed. A company raid, for instance, called for twenty men, including one officer. All would go to back areas and study air photos of enemy trenches and rehearse the job, with each man assigned a special role. If it was to be a stealth raid, they would blacken their faces and, when the time came, crawl out in the darkness to cut wire and slither through the gap. One clumsy move and a vigilant enemy could wipe out the lot; success hung on not only one's own stealth, but that of all the others. However, if they caught the enemy napping the results were satisfying. The reliable stalkers soon became known and they made themselves familiar with enemy habits by careful observation. No wonder the Germans likened them to Red Indians and grew to fear them.

Another type of raid was advertised. Again at night, with faces blackened, the raiding party got into position in no-man's-land just before zero hour. A barrage was turned on the enemy by artillery and machine-guns, to prevent the bringing up of reinforcements. At the same time, an advance group of raiders started forward with a bangalore torpedo—an iron tube eight or ten feet long stuffed with high explosive—to blow a gap in the barbed wire. This whole operation had to be exactly timed to catch the Germans still in their dugouts, sheltering from shells when the raiders reached their trenches. The leading files carried rifles, bayonets and explosives to throw in the dugouts.

Divisional raids were on a grand scale, sometimes with gas. Then whole battalions would be taken out of the line to train for them.

Such operations were usually carried out on "a quiet front"; that is, where no battle was in progress. The rewards were valuable—prisoners, information, the destruction of enemy tunnels and mines, the damage to German morale. They also served to relieve the awful tedium of trench life with its mud, stench and vermin. So skilful and proficient did the Canadians become in the art, that in 1916 the French army detached officers, N.C.O.'s and men from the famous *Chasseurs à pied* to practise with Canadian raiding parties.

With raids such as these the only diversion, the winter of 1915-16 was a misery. Bitter winds and continuing rains made it far worse than Salisbury Plain, for there were none of the amenities of the camp in England. In the absence of major engagements the troops spent the time maintaining trenches and breastworks that liquefied and dissolved in the rain. Water rose thigh-deep and the high rubber waders that had been ordered the year before did not arrive till the following spring, when the need was far less urgent. Illness was prevalent and the continual wetness induced a painful condition known as trench feet, similar to frost-bite. If neglected, it could turn to gangrene.

The padres in the Chaplain Service could do much for morale. In the first years before the Salvation Army and Y.M.C.A. got going, the padres rounded up entertainment and social activities behind the lines, visited hospitals and casualty clearing stations, served hot coffee to chilled soldiers in the line, wrote next-of-kin. Church services were of lesser importance. A padre's value was judged, not by the number of men he approached, but by the number who voluntarily sought him.

In that war cleanliness was not next to godliness. The men of God who served their Master best were in the front lines. Filthy and fearful like the fighting men, they buried the dead, comforted the dying, endured with the living. Men of all faiths served courageously. Perhaps the best known and best loved was the senior chaplain, Frederick George Scott, C.M.G., D.S.O. Canon Scott was a poet and scholar. Born in Montreal in 1861, he was fifty-three years old when he went overseas with the 1st Division and he spent most of his time with his men in forward areas. Brutinel remembers with a chuckle that he bestowed an accumulation of blessings on the 1st Motors in what he called celestial compensation for the free loan of motor transport to the front.

Canon Scott shared in his men's bloody battles. After an action his lonely wraith-like figure could be seen searching the battlefield for the wounded, collecting "dog-tags" from the dead and giving them

Christian burial. His own son was killed in 1916 and he searched no-man's-land in vain for his body. He himself was wounded in 1918.

There were many fine padres, and to mention some is to omit others as worthy, but chaplains were killed, wounded and taken prisoner with their men, and they earned their awards for valour.

That winter a third division was formed in England and a fourth promised. Colonel Mercer (1st Brigade) was promoted and named G.O.C. of the new division which included as part of the 7th Brigade the P.P.C.L.I. (after a year of distinction with the British 27th) and the only Permanent Force battalion, the Royal Canadian Regiment, fresh from a year of guard duty in Bermuda.

At British G.H.Q. Sir Douglas Haig replaced Sir John French as Commander-in-Chief.

In February, 1916, the 1st and 2nd Divisions moved back to the bloody salient of Ypres, a battleground since 1914. There they acted in close co-operation with the British, holding a line from Hooge, south to St. Eloi. The countryside was desolate—spikes and stumps of trees marked former green woods, the ground a lumpy mass of churned mud and shell-holes. Small streams, their natural courses destroyed, found any low level including the trenches men were occupying.

The 2nd Division was to relieve the British after the success of an operation planned for March 27. The object was to cut off the enemy-held salient at St. Eloi, a slight knoll or mound in a water-logged area where the Patricias had fought desperately the year before.

For six months British engineers had been tunnelling, sinking shafts as deep as sixty feet, running galleries under the German positions and cramming them with explosives. The theory behind this undertaking was that the Germans would be blown to bits and the British could walk in and take over the line, reversing the salient and advancing as much as three hundred yards. Then the Canadian 2nd Division would relieve the British and hold the line.

So much for the plan. Unhappily, those responsible gave no thought to the resulting condition of the ground over which the British must advance.

On the morning of March 27 the mines were fired and the German front line exploded. Tons of mud and debris rose high in the air, descended to annihilate enemy troops and lines. Trenches on both fronts collapsed, familiar landmarks were obliterated. Seven or more huge craters were formed, the largest 50 feet deep and 180 feet across. Any remaining drainage system was demolished; the craters became lakes, every shell-hole a pond, what remained of former trenches held three or more feet of water.

The British made a temporary advance and occupied three craters, but their reserve line no longer existed and no one realized that the unoccupied craters constituted great gaps in their defences. The Germans soon discovered this and moved in.

There was no success for the British. Exhausted, for a whole week they held on, capturing all but the German key-point. They fought in the most appalling conditions, crouching in mud or standing waist-deep in water, under constant shelling with no relief or rest. Too often the wounded drowned where they dropped.

Plans were advanced. The Canadians were ordered to take over before the line was stabilized. With only half of them in steel helmets —there were not enough to go round—the 2nd Division moved in on April 4.

Work parties tried to construct new trenches, but supplies could not be brought up through the morass of mud and the raking fire of concentrated enemy guns. Machine-gunners, man-handling their guns and ammunition, manned their posts, but communications were cut and the altered landscape, with no recognizable landmarks, was confusing and misleading. Guns jammed in the mud or sank in the bog.

When the Germans attacked, effective resistance was impossible. Momentarily a section of the assault was held up by crossfire from the 31st Battalion's guns, but the German sweep wiped out one machine-gun post after another.

The situation was almost intolerable and the two Canadian generals, Alderson and Turner, agreed that the attack should be made on a wider front, reducing the concentration of men, now such a good target for enemy artillery. But when General Alderson made the proposal to the Army Commander, General Plumer, he, in a mistaken appraisal of the situation, ordered the Canadians to hold their position and recover the German-held craters. This was more easily ordered than done. The craters were designated by numbers but only aerial observation (unavailable because of bad weather) could have established which crater was held by whom, and this confusion cost the Division dearly.

For two more weeks they were pounded by concentrated artillery and machine-guns, yet the Canadians held their ground and doggedly fought back. It was still the old story—men against guns. In the end both sides reverted to static warfare. Thousands died, from gun fire or drowning, and little was accomplished by the whole terrible engagement. But the insignificance of the gains cannot detract from the incredible bravery and stoicism of the 2nd Division in this ill-conceived action. Canadian casualties were nearly three times those of the Germans, and the slaughter had all been over the ownership of seven holes in the mud.

The battle of the St. Eloi Craters left a bad taste. British G.H.Q., as a matter of principle, searched for a scapegoat; had difficulty in agreeing on whom to blame. Sir Max Aitken (later Lord Beaverbrook), who held the impressive title of General Representative of Canada at the Front, cabled Sir Sam Hughes that the British "viewed the error as serious." General Plumer ordered Alderson to remove Brigadier General Ketchen (6th Canadian Brigade). General Turner (2nd Division, of which the 6th was a part) refused to comply with the order, so Alderson asked to have Turner removed. The Commander-in-Chief, General Haig, refused to remove Turner, and for the time being all three officers retained their commands. However Sir Max and Sir Douglas had a long interview at which, according to Aitken, Haig "stipulated that Canada should give him the assistance required in disposing of General Alderson."

Sir Max made the recommendation in a cable to Sir Sam, and the Corps Commander was made Inspector General of Canadian Forces in England. Alderson had done a difficult and commendable job, but the Corps was suffering from a clash of personalities and he was the one to go.

Meanwhile no one gave thought to the expert who originally advocated blowing a major volcano on a narrow front in low-lying marshland, and the 2nd Division, in their first major action, received small credit for their enduring resistance and fortitude in the fortnight's ordeal.

6

SANCTUARY WOOD AND THE BATTLE OF MOUNT SORREL

Lieutenant-General the Honourable Sir Julian Byng succeeded General Alderson as Corps Commander on May 29, 1916. He was ideally suited to command the individualistic men from the Dominion, for he had led irregulars in the South African War and was no slave to orthodoxy or dogma. He quickly sized up the Canadians for what they were—intelligent, hard-fighting men of action, and the Canadians responded to his approbation.

Although the month of May saw no major activity, the Corps suffered a couple of thousand casualties, mostly from shells and machine-guns. This was nothing new, for the Germans still had overwhelming superiority in fire-power, but a significant step forward was made that month.

Currie had been warned that soon they would be moving north to the most easterly projection of the Ypres Salient. Here they would relieve British troops who had taken terrible punishment from the exposed flank, and the general felt that something could be done to cut down losses. Sending for Brutinel, Currie ordered him to make a careful survey of the area and report on prevailing conditions.

Brutinel, with one of his officers, Captain Lionel Francis, arrived at British Brigade Headquarters early one morning. They received a chilly welcome from the brigadier general.

The Canadian made his mission known and asked for a guided tour of the trenches and back areas, only to receive a curt reply.

"No one is allowed to move in the salient by daylight, and I won't risk the lives of any of my men," said the general. "You may try at your own risk, but I've warned you."

This ended the brief interview.

The colonel and Captain Francis proceeded with their task; they spent most of the day studying the ground and locating projected strong-points on their maps. The day was quiet, the weather fine and there was no trouble till late afternoon.

They were studying a map on the edge of a shell-hole when suddenly Francis exclaimed:

"Don't move sir! They might shoot!"

Half a dozen burly British soldiers were covering them with fixed bayonets. They had been detailed, they said, to arrest the spies who had been going around all day releasing pigeons.

In the midst of explaining that the pigeons were actually a covey of partridges, three times disturbed, a short sharp bombardment compelled them all to shelter in the same shell-hole. Then, with discreet docility, the two spies accompanied the warriors back to the captain who had sent them out. He accepted their explanation, but seemed glad to see them go.

The reconnaissance revealed that the front-line trenches were in bad shape; most of them too shallow. The areas adjacent to the support lines had been ignored and as far as could be seen or learned, no strong-points had been considered. The British troops in that particular sector stoically suffered needlessly heavy casualties.

General Currie asked Major-General W. B. Lindsay, Chief Engineer, to discuss this with Brutinel and make necessary plans to improve the front-line areas and machine-gun strong-points. A company of pioneers and machine-gunners worked together. Railway ties were laid flat on the water-soaked ground and capped with steel rails, roofing all machine-gun emplacements and as many of the dugouts as possible.

When the 1st and 3rd Divisions took over by the end of the month, conditions were considerably improved and casualties sharply reduced from those suffered by the British. This was to pay a high dividend in the imminent battles of Sanctuary Wood and Mount Sorrel.

June 1 found the two Divisions in place on the crest of the Ypres Ridge, the 3rd Division on the right of the 1st, and both expecting a serious German attack. The 1st and 4th Canadian Mounted Rifles occupied several knolls, among them Mount Sorrel and Tor Top, while the P.P.C.L.I. were lined up on the left at a lower level in Sanctuary Wood. Patrols had reported that the Germans were digging saps, and aerial photos showed a layout well behind enemy lines, which closely resembled the Canadian positions. This indicated rehearsal for an assault.

On the following day the Germans let fly with the worst bombardment yet experienced by the Canadians. No believers in the superiority of man over the machine, the Germans had been steadily increasing the size and concentration of the artillery barrages. The 3rd Division took the full force, and during the attack lost its leader when General Mercer was killed. The commander of the 8th Brigade, Brigadier General Williams, who was with him on a reconnaissance, was wounded and captured.

The intense artillery fire continued all morning. Just after noon, the Germans exploded mines in front of the Canadian trenches. Then came waves of grey-coated infantrymen with bayonets, bombs and flame-throwers. Two veteran battalions, the Patricias (3rd Division) and the 5th Battalion (1st Division) raked the attackers with machine-gun fire, but nothing halted the methodical organized advance. They captured strong-points and overran a section of the 5th Battery, Canadian Field Artillery, killing or wounding all the gunners. A German historian wrote later ". . . here too, the Canadians did not surrender, but at their guns, defended themselves with revolvers to the last man."

This was the only occasion in the war when the field guns of the Canadian Corps fell into German hands. The two 18-pounders were recovered in the subsequent fighting.

The Germans never understood the initiative of the individual Canadian private soldier and his stubborn resistance in the face of certain defeat. German soldiers and junior officers, surrounded and out of touch with directives, usually surrendered. Native cussedness made the Canadian fight to the bitter end—or win his way back to his own lines.

At Sanctuary Wood the Patricias again covered themselves with glory. One of their two companies was overrun; the second escaped the worst of the bombardment and fired into the enemy's right rear.

Isolated, it held out for eighteen hours when all officers had been killed or wounded. In the rear, the other two Patricia companies bore the brunt of the fighting, beating off German penetration.

This battle cost the regiment four hundred casualties and the death of their commanding officer, Lieutenant-Colonel H. C. Buller. Originally 90 per cent British-born veterans, it was by then manned by specially recruited replacements from Canadian university companies, and they acquitted themselves as ably and courageously as had their predecessors.

On the previous day, for the first time since its arrival in France nearly a year before, the 1st Canadian Motor Machine Gun Brigade had been withdrawn from the line for a short rest in Poperinghe, as Corps reserves. Their rest was brief.

Next morning Brutinel, with a leave warrant in his pocket, decided to visit the Corps back areas. Accompanied by an N.C.O., he left at daybreak, arrived on the Corps lines, and proceeded towards the southern boundary of the 1st Division, near the bend of the Ypres Canal. All was quiet. Suddenly about eight o'clock the massed artillery bombardment began, extending from the front line to about eight miles behind Ypres. Gas shells were frequent.

Three or four hours later, abruptly, it stopped. The sudden silence, in its own way, was for the moment almost unbearable. The two men, miraculously, were unharmed except for the N.C.O. whose gas mask was in bad shape. Practically blinded by fumes, Brutinel led him to safety; then, filled with misgivings, he went to the nearest headquarters, where he was welcomed by General Lipsett, now commander of the 2nd Brigade.

According to Lipsett, the situation could not have been worse. General Mercer was dead; several brigadiers were believed dead or captured; front-line trenches and their occupants had been annihilated and whole units almost wiped out. Communications with the front and with Divisional Headquarters had been destroyed. The 3rd Division, which had taken the brunt of the attack, was now leaderless, and the 4th Canadian Mounted Rifles had suffered over six hundred casualties, leaving a gap of 600 yards through which the Germans could attack Ypres unmolested. Lipsett doubted there were sufficient reinforcements to fill the breach in time.

Brutinel suggested that the 1st Motors, withdrawn the day before, could go forward to secure the flank of the 2nd Brigade. His men knew the territory well, giving them an advantage. The road from

Poperinghe to Ypres was under steady bombardment, but he was confident they could get through.

General Lipsett welcomed the suggestion, and agreed to inform Canadian Corps Headquarters that the Motor Machine Gun Brigade had been engaged to meet the emergency.

Brutinel got a message through to his brigade, but it was nearly midnight when he met "A" and "B" Batteries at the Lille Gate in Ypres. He explained the situation to his officers and ordered the batteries to deploy and establish contact with the enemy all along the reported gap, up to and including Zillebeke. By four a.m. they reported back that they had made contact with German scouts and patrols, but that Zillebeke was in Canadian hands.

A counter-attack was scheduled for that morning all along the line. The signal to start was to be six simultaneous rockets, but so many rockets misfired that the uneven discharge confused the infantry, some of whom never even saw them. Over open ground, in broad daylight and against a hail of machine-gun fire, there was little chance of success. Men of the 3rd Brigade reformed on the Motors' lines, digging shallow trenches for themselves. The dismounted guns of the Motors, placed at tactical points, gave protection and plugged a 600-yard gap.

During the course of that day a signal came from Corps H.Q. telling Brutinel to withdraw at once and return the Motors to Corps Reserve. Obviously, this order could not be obeyed—the infantry could not be left unprotected. Brutinel saw Brigadier General Tuxford of the 3rd Brigade, who was busily engaged on the centre front, and told him he had disregarded orders from Corps H.Q. to withdraw. Tuxford gratefully commended him.

The situation did not improve, but next day a second signal from Army Corps arrived with a peremptory order to withdraw at once and report to Corps H.Q. Again Brutinel ignored the order, confident that the Corps Commander could not be properly informed of the situation. But on the third day when a new order arrived, there was no mention of the Motors withdrawing; Brutinel himself was to report personally to Corps H.Q. The summons was ominous.

Calling General Lipsett on the field telephone, Brutinel asked him if he had advised Corps H.Q. of the whereabouts of the Motors, the reason and the emergency. General Lipsett replied he had tried, but was not certain the message had been delivered. He was not comforting.

Brutinel realized he could be in serious trouble. He went off to 1st Division H.Q., hoping to have the sympathetic ear of General Currie, but the General was in the lines when he arrived. Brutinel explained the situation to the General Staff Officer, Colonel Kinsley, who did his best to reassure him.

"We appreciate what you've done, Bruty," he said. "No matter what happens the 1st Division stands behind you. I'm sure the Corps Commander, when he knows the facts, will change his attitude."

Encouraged, Brutinel went on to Corps H.Q. to face the music and try to explain why he took it upon himself to move and engage his unit, like an independent commander with a private army.

He was received by Brigadier General de B. Radcliffe, General Staff, who looked sternly at the errant colonel.

"It's too bad you didn't obey the order when you first received it. You'll have to explain to the Corps Commander. He'll see you in a moment."

Lieutenant-General Sir Julian Byng had assumed his command only a few days before. Having just returned from the Dardanelles campaign, it can be assumed that his association with Canadians had been slight. He received Brutinel at once.

General Byng said coldly: "Here is a map of the front. Please explain the present position as far as you know it."

Conversant with current conditions, the colonel was able to describe them in detail. It was a grim story. Byng listened intently, then said: "Now explain why you failed to obey my orders. A battle was in progress, and the only reserves I had were engaged without my knowledge."

Brutinel recounted events as he knew them from that morning of June 2: the devastating three-hour bombardment; General Lipsett's concern and his news of the lost commanders; the plight of the 3rd Division; the gap that left the front wide open and the lack of reinforcements.

Lipsett, he told General Byng, had seized on the suggestion of using the Motors to fill the gap, but the message to Headquarters telling of the emergency had never been delivered. Later on, receiving the order to withdraw, he had consulted General Tuxford who agreed that to comply would leave the infantry without support, severely damage their morale, and jeopardize the whole line. In consequence, Brutinel felt that he had no alternative but to stay.

General Byng listened quietly while Brutinel made his explanation, then rising, he placed both hands on the machine-gunner's shoulders and said emphatically: "Had you not done as you did, I would have had you court-martialed. Now Brutinel, what are your plans?"

The tension relieved, the Canadian outlined his proposal to leave the Motors with the infantry until the lost ground had been recovered. Byng concurred, nodding his approval, as together they discussed the details. As he was leaving Brutinel, patting his pocket, smiled.

"It's a good way to spend my leave," he said.

"Leave!" exclaimed Sir Julian. Turning to his staff officer, the Corps Commander continued; "What sort of fools have we got here? Officers with leave warrants in their pockets, staying instead to fight battles!" He turned back to Brutinel. "Are there many officers of that kind in the Canadian Corps?"

"Most of our officers would have done as I did," was the reply.

General Byng was impressed with this opinion of his new command.

"I think we've struck it rich," he said to General Radcliffe.

Brutinel returned to the front where the Canadians were still engaged in desperate fighting for the Salient. They were badly in need of reinforcements after the staggering losses of the first days in June, but Sir Douglas Haig, busily engaged in preparations for the Somme offensive, was unwilling to divert his troops. Ironically, he suggested instead, what he considered second best—the substitution of artillery for infantry.

Massed guns of the Canadian Corps, the Lahore (Indian) Division, the British and South African Artillery, pounded the enemy lines inflicting "horrifying losses" according to German accounts, and greatly hampering their consolidation of previous gains. By June 13 the Canadians had recovered much of the old line. The enemy, after a couple of unsuccessful counter-attacks, called off the battle. This successful experiment of substituting machines for manpower seemed to make no impression on Higher Command thinking.

After the battles of the St. Eloi Craters, Sanctuary Wood and Mount Sorrel, Prime Minister Asquith questioned Haig about the Canadian casualties and the advisability of holding the Ypres Salient. The *Private Papers of Douglas Haig, 1914-1919* contain this entry in his diary for June 7 (1916): ". . . I easily satisfied them as to why it was necessary to hold on to the Salient and the causes of the casualties among Canadians. Incidentally I reproved Bonar Law for listening to some pluckless Canadians who had urged on him the abandonment of the Ypres Salient."

The Canadians, like General Smith-Dorrien a year before, had urged the abandonment of this sodden bulge, dominated on three sides by the enemy. They understood the tactical importance of ground in fighting a battle. But Haig never seemed to grasp it, and in consequence hundreds of thousands of young men from all parts of the British Empire died needlessly.

June ended in a mood of depression. In addition to the reverses, the Allied world mourned what seemed to many a national calamity. On June 5, Field Marshal Lord Kitchener, Secretary of State for War and a heroic figure since the capture of Omdurman in the Sudan, 1898, sailed from Scapa Flow aboard the H.M.S. *Hampshire* for Archangel. The Tsar of Russia had invited him to criticize and counsel his military authorities. Near the Shetland Islands the *Hampshire* struck a mine and sank with nearly all hands.

But worse was ahead. On July 1 the Battle of the Somme began, lasted five months, and was one of the greatest blood-baths in history.

7

THE BATTLES OF THE SOMME

One of Sir Julian Byng's first duties, after he took command of the Canadians, was to find a commander for the 3rd Division to replace General Mercer. Among the brigadiers from whom he could choose was Garnet Hughes, son of the Minister of Militia, who eight months before had been given the 1st Brigade on his father's orders. The news of General Mercer's death had hardly reached Canada when General Byng received a curt cable from Ottawa saying "Give Garnet 3rd Division" and signed "Sam."

No doubt Sir Julian and Brigadier General de B. Radcliffe had a very good idea who Garnet and Sam were, but the Corps Commander chose to ignore the message, and the command of the 3rd went to General Lipsett. Two weeks with the Canadians in action had impressed General Byng with their fighting ability, but there is reason to believe he had doubts about the men behind the men behind the guns.

Administrative confusion was considerable. Reinforcements were already a problem, yet fifth and sixth divisions were being considered, ignoring the growing need for reinforcements necessitated by the increasing casualties. There was interference at all levels from England and Canada, and long delays on recommendations sent in for promotion. Scores of huge packing cases clogged Corps H.Q. containing thousands of personal letters from Canada inquiring about individual soldiers. Orders from Canada required that all such letters be answered. Byng put his foot down on such nonsense. The problem at hand was solved by an opportune fire in headquarters that destroyed the lot.

But under General Byng organization and harmony prevailed at Corps level and were soon reflected in the discipline and co-operation of all branches of the Force. Infantry, artillery, engineers, signallers, supply troops—all pulled their weight, and none more than the Medical Corps.

In England the Canadian Army Medical Corps was the subject of criticism, investigation and controversy by Canadians in the first years, but in France there was nothing but praise. The regimental medical officer kept men fit in the line, and followed them into battle. In existing conditions the absence of typhoid was almost miraculous, due to the rigid precautions in purifying all sources of drinking water and inoculation. Stretcher-bearers, as the months progressed, became experts in first aid and performed Herculean feats carrying stretchers through knee-deep porridge-like mud. Nursing sisters worked long hours, sometimes in canvas-covered casualty clearing stations or in the open. In the rainy seasons they often worked in wet clothing, and after heavy fighting they might be on duty around the clock or catnap under damp blankets.

The Canadians remained in the Ypres Salient all summer, in official parlance "stationary yet aggressive." This meant no major operations but continual harassment of the enemy with raids, mines, and bombardment. In the summer of 1915, the 1st Division had been relieved of that aid-to-the-enemy, the Ross rifle. In the summer of 1916 they were entirely withdrawn, the other divisions receiving Lee-Enfields too. The Colt machine-guns also disappeared, to be replaced with Vickers, and the infantry were issued with Lewis machine-guns, much lighter and more easily handled weapons.

The 4th Division officially arrived in France that summer but certain of its battalions were veteran units and had seen bitter fighting in the Salient the spring before. The other machine-gun batteries arrived in France that summer too, and Byng grouped the five batteries—two Sifton, the Borden, Eaton, and Yukon—under Brutinel's command. Byng, receptive to new ideas, had become a strong advocate of Brutinel's theories of machine-gun employment.

Meanwhile the British went into action on the Somme on July 1 with no other strategical objective than to relieve pressure on the French at Verdun, where the German offensive was already petering out. Haig's policy was to "wear down" the German forces, but in the process the British were worn down too, and on that first day suffered 57,470 casualties. At Beaumont-Hamel the Newfoundland Regiment, at nine a.m. on July 1, advanced over the same ground where, earlier that day, two previous assaults had failed. In a matter of minutes 715 Newfoundlanders fell, hung up on barbed wire and riddled with machine-gun fire. In the first two months only a few hundred yards were gained at the cost of 200,000 British casualties.

The Canadians relieved the Australians in early September. The 1st Division was to hold a quiet front of 3,000 yards while the 2nd and 3rd Divisions prepared for a grand assault, scheduled for September 15. However it takes two to make a quiet front, and in the three days under heavy fire and repeated counter-attacks the 1st Division had nearly a thousand casualties.

The Battle of Flers-Courcelette started on schedule and was remarkable because it introduced a new weapon, the tank. On the 14th, Colonel Brutinel received orders to report to General Byng's headquarters. The Corps Commander greeted him with a broad smile.

"Bruty," he said, "I have a little present for you."

The colonel registered his surprise; presents from corps commanders were uncommon.

"You will go to the goods station at Amiens," continued Sir Julian. "There you will find some tanks which have been sent us for trial."

"You mean water-tanks, sir?"

"Not exactly! They're a war secret. Have a look at them and let me know how we can use them."

The tank idea had been conceived as early as 1914 in the mind of a forward-thinking British officer, Lieutenant-Colonel E. D. Swinton, one of those who had recognized the murderous effectiveness of the machine-gun. He failed to interest the War Office, but by 1915, when enemy guns were wiping out British lives by the thousands, he took his idea to Winston Churchill, First Lord of the Admiralty, whose active and imaginative brain saw the possibilities of a "machine-gun destroyer"—an armoured vehicle that could attack machine-gun emplacements, through wire and over shell-holes and trenches.

Although the War Office regarded it with distaste, the tank was born —a weapon with the prime purpose of combating enemy machine-gun nests. The first ones were 26½ feet long, nearly 14 feet wide and more than 7 feet high, with tracks instead of wheels. Attached to each was a six-foot tail with two heavy wheels in the rear. This was to minimize shock, and also acted as a sort of rudder or drag, with the double purpose of steering and braking. Under first-class conditions they had a maximum speed of 3.7 miles per hour. Being protégés of the Admiralty they were first named land-cruisers, or land-ships. The name "tank" was used for security to mislead informers. As they were armed with Vickers and Hotchkiss machine-guns (later "male" tanks carried two six-pounder guns as well) they were known as Machine Gun Corps, Heavy Section, to be employed in support of attacking infantry.

General Haig was over-eager to try them out, for by the end of August his bloody campaign on the Somme badly needed a victory. He brought pressure to bear on the War Office, and against the judgment of those concerned, forty-eight tanks were delivered to the front by the middle of September. Colonel Swinton had prepared a pamphlet on their tactical employment, but this was ignored. Like the earlier misuse of the machine-guns, the tanks too were misused, and because of their disappointing performance they were almost discarded. More than a year passed before they were used correctly.

The tanks allotted to the Canadians were attached to the 1st Motors for rations and supplies, and at the Amiens railway station on September 14, 1916, Colonel Brutinel saw them for the first time.

He looked them over critically while the major in charge explained their function and described their reaction to various tests. Brutinel doubted if the tests had been severe enough, but suggested that the major come with him to look over the ground near Pozières—the jumping-off line.

It was a long way from Amiens to Pozières, a long way that is for vehicles slower than foot soldiers. After looking over the area, the major agreed it would be hard to have them on the jumping-off line at zero hour, but he would try. If successful, the tanks would then do their best to support the attacking troops, even though their speed under battle conditions would be considerably less than that of the infantry.

Brutinel reported to General Byng, describing the vehicles and their intended employment provided they reached the area in time. Privately, he felt that their use was premature, before mechanical faults were eradicated, and the limited number would achieve little.

He was right, for many miles of trial and demonstrations had almost worn them out. In the cratered ground, mechanical failures were terribly high. Six started with the Canadians. Creeping snailwise into battle they were sitting ducks for enemy shell-fire, yet heavy barrages from German machine-guns splattered harmlessly on the armour of those still mobile. Their steady if slow advance created a panic which brought the surrender of many Germans. Certainly they were morale-builders to British troops generally, except for a small group of unfortunate infantrymen who were detailed, five to each tank, to walk in front and remove casualties from their path. They shared the spotlight without benefit of armour, and their enthusiasm for the new secret weapon must have been dubious.

Of the six tanks assigned to the Canadians, only one reached the objective, actively supporting the infantry in the capture of the sugar refinery at Courcelette, a strongly defended German strong-point. The others broke down, turned over in shell-holes, or were knocked out by artillery. Later there was considerable mechanical improvement, but it was not until the last six months of the war that the Higher Command fully grasped their proper function and use.

In this first action, however, for the first time in two sordid months of slaughter, Sir Douglas Haig had an intoxicating sip of success, and promptly asked the War Office for a thousand tanks. Then as sobriety returned, enthusiasm waned.

Tanks were in short supply. Those available, to the heartbreak and despair of the officers of the Heavy Branch, were used in the worst possible way tactically—in penny packets, often over swamp-land, consolidating gains made by the infantry. Instead they should have been employed as breakthrough weapons, in mass formation and in depth over firm ground, with the infantry consolidating *their* gains.

Courcelette was captured on September 15 by the Canadian 5th Brigade, which at dusk took the Germans by surprise and stormed through the town in ugly street-fighting. The French-Canadian 22nd Battalion made a name for their regiment by their discipline, skill and courage, fighting off fourteen counter-attacks and flushing Germans from cellars and dugouts. They captured a bag of prisoners, including two doctors, and two officers who said they were noblemen —one a count, the other a baron. Both these officers objected to being taken back in company with prisoners of lower rank, and worried lest their own guns fire on them in the process. Lieutenant-Colonel

Tremblay, C.O of the 22nd, sent them back vigorously waving a Red Cross flag, but the Germans fired on them anyway and the whole party had to take shelter in shell-holes. The noblemen got away temporarily, but were caught and spent the rest of the war as prisoners. In contrast, the two doctors tended the wounded of both sides and earned the respect of their captors.

Fierce fighting took place along the whole line, but the effectiveness of indirect machine-gun fire was evident and encouraged the Canadian infantryman. The Lewis gunners went forward with the infantry, and the brigade machine-gun companies manned strongpoints; although these were the focus of enemy artillery, they poured streams of bullets into the Germans by direct and indirect fire.

Lieutenant-Colonel C. S. Grafton in his history of the Canadian Machine Gun Corps (*The Canadian "Emma Gees"*) deplores the curtness of the machine-gun companies' reports. He writes: "Apparently the new formation, while they believed they were fighting a war to end all war, had no notion that they were also supposed to do a little writing for posterity." But they were too busy to do much writing or worrying about posterity. The Suicide Club, they were called, and their reports were written in blood, but in the Canadian Corps reports, along with the 1st Canadian Motor Machine Gun Brigade, they received special mention for initiative and audacity.

The 3rd Division took heavy punishment, but they too discharged their assignment. Although the main objectives were yet to be taken, Sir Douglas Haig, in his dispatches, wrote that "the gains made by the Canadians were more considerable than any which had attended our arms in the course of a single operation, since the commencement of the offensive."

By now the bad weather was setting in. The Corps was allotted the task of capturing Kenora and Regina trenches, heavily defended lines on a crest with a full view of Allied rear areas. In spite of almost incessant artillery fire, enemy wire remained uncut and their trenches undamaged. Thus, on September 26, waves of men of the 1st Division found themselves hung up on solid barbed-wire entanglements, caught in withering hostile fire from artillery and machine-gun nests.

In spite of this Kenora Trench was captured; but in the next twelve hours it was lost, recaptured, and lost again. Attacks and counterattacks went on for three days, virtually over the same slippery muddy ground, and bitter hand-to-hand fighting took place in the pelting rain.

On October 1 the 3rd Division tried again. The attempt failed, and the 4th and 5th Canadian Mounted Rifles endured what practically amounted to massacre. Finally most of Kenora was taken but Regina remained almost untouched, its defences unscathed. On the 8th, another heartbreaking assault was made. About one hundred Highlanders of the 16th Battalion, inspired by eighteen-year-old Piper James Richardson, who "strode up and down . . . playing his pipes with the greatest coolness," somehow reached Regina Trench. But their numbers were too few to hold it. Piper Richardson, missing and presumed killed, was awarded a posthumous Victoria Cross.

Greater accuracy of indirect fire by heavy artillery came later in the war, but according to Lieutenant-Colonel A. G. L. McNaughton, then commanding the 11th Brigade, Canadian Field Artillery, it was a "disheartening task endeavouring to cut wire with field gun shrapnel." Heavy shells were not being used. They were in short supply; besides, it was thought the resulting craters would be an obstacle to the infantry.

By October 17 most of the Canadian Corps had moved out of the Somme sector. Left were the Corps artillery, the 1st Motors, and the 4th Division which came into the line on October 10. This was the newest division and was to operate with the 2nd British Corps under General Sir Hubert Gough's Fifth Army.

The weather became progressively worse—trenches knee-deep in water, all semblance of dugouts destroyed by shells or rain. On October 21 the 4th Division attacked Regina behind a creeping barrage of their own, this time with partial success. Persistent bombardment had at last cut the wire and destroyed the trench: the 11th Brigade occupied part but not all of the objective. Four days later the 44th Battalion made what was hoped would be the final assault on the rest of Regina Trench, only to be forced back and almost annihilated by a heavy defensive barrage.

Further action was repeatedly postponed by the weather, but at midnight on November 10-11 the 10th and 11th Brigades attacked. This time all went well, and in less than two hours all of Regina was in the hands of the Canadians, and their gains consolidated. But it was a hollow victory. Once a strong position, it was now smashed and flattened by repeated bombardment—a mass of debris and dead bodies, too many of them Canadian.

General Gough, optimistic with this hard-won success, decided to resume the offensive in the face of worsening weather conditions, conflicting intelligence reports, and too hopeful and too hasty preparations. This time the Canadian objective was Desire Trench and the support trenches several hundred yards north of Regina. Conditions could not have been much worse. Soaked and coated with mud, men's clothing was so sodden as to add over fifty pounds to their carrying weight. The wet kilts of Highland battalions froze and cut their knees. Long sopping greatcoats froze, knocked against ankles and tripped their wearers. Men who solved that problem by hacking them off at the knees were threatened with charge of "wilfully damaging His Majesty's property." Others tied or pinned up the corners with safety pins from their "housewife" sewing kits.

The attack started early on the morning of November 18. Snow had fallen in the night, changed to sleet and finally to rain. With a blanket of snow over freezing mud, it was not only hard to find direction, but the artillery was too unsure of the infantry's whereabouts to maintain support. Only raw courage and endurance sustained the men of the 4th Division. The 11th Brigade achieved their objective and more, capturing the required trenches and pushing beyond to establish machine-gun posts. Unfortunately, the flanking battalions had been forced back by merciless machine-gun fire. The British, too, had failed to reach their objective, and little was gained, although the Canadians captured over six hundred prisoners in the day's fighting.

This was the last action for the Canadians on the Somme that fall. On November 28, when the 4th Division moved out to join the rest of the Corps on the Lens-Arras front, after some seven weeks in the line, it had proved its mettle as a fighting division.

Too many Canadians stayed on, never to leave. Casualties totalled more than 24,000, a staggering price to pay for nothing more than the knowledge that the Germans, after all, were not invincible. Two years of war and the cream of a generation, volunteers all, had been spilt on the fields of France and Flanders.

8

ADMINISTRATION DIFFICULTIES AND PREPARATION FOR THE SPRING OFFENSIVE

During 1915, Canadian Administration in England had grown into a multi-headed monster made up of senior officials, civil and military, all bickering and vying for authority over Canadian forces. Major-Generals S. B. Steele and J. W. Carson, Brigadier Generals J. C. McDougall and Lord Brooke, the Acting Canadian High Commissioner Sir George Perley, and certainly not least Sir Max Aitken, all carried on independent correspondence with the Canadian government, War Office, and Corps H.Q. in France. Often they countermanded each other's orders.

General Steele deserves special mention, for he was a veteran officer of the old Northwest Mounted Police, served in the Fenian Raids, the Riel Rebellion, commanded the Strathcona's in the South African War, raised and trained the 2nd Division and took it to England. At one time Hughes had opposed Steele as G.O.C. 2nd Division, but when Kitchener, who favoured an Imperial commander, also objected on the grounds that "to do justice to the troops very experienced officers" were necessary, Sir Sam protested heatedly. Kitchener's objection was hardly justified in view of Steele's background, but the old warrior was now sixty-six years old. Hughes and Kitchener compromised by giving the command to General Turner, and Steele was put in command of the Shorncliffe area, now replacing Salisbury Plain as a training ground for Canadian troops.

Appeals to Canada to resolve the farcical administration situation brought Sir Sam Hughes to England in March 1916. There he authorized Sir Max as chairman to set up what he called an "informal council." The subsequent committee was composed of the recalcitrant generals and was to meet weekly, deal with military matters, and refer non-military questions to the Acting High Commissioner. Simultaneously, in Canada, the Chief of General Staff, Major-General W. G. Gwatkin, advised Sir Robert Borden to make his own plans for a *not*-so-informal overseas council. This the Prime Minister did, intending to appoint Sir George Perley president with representatives of senior members of the General Staff in Canada. But Hughes, on his return from England, finally convinced Sir Robert that his plan was better.

It wasn't.

At the two meetings held, no two members agreed. Sir Max refused to attend either meeting because all would not agree with him—or as he called it, co-operate. He reported to Hughes: "I decided on my own account to place every obstacle in the way of the formation of that committee and this I have done." No further meetings were held.

Contention existed between Borden and Hughes as to the personnel of such a committee, for Sir Robert wanted an overseas council whose first consideration and loyalty would be to the cabinet, not the Minister of Militia. The High Commissioner was the logical person to head it, but Perley was a long-time enemy of Hughes and the Minister would have none of him. Once again Borden sent him overseas to set up another committee—warning him beforehand that any appointments must be approved and passed by Order-in-Council before formal authorization.

Once again Hughes set up his council—somewhat enlarged but still comprised of the same old gang and the same chairman. It operated for three months before the government learned of it from the press, along with the rest of the world. Hughes was ordered home.

Sir Sam seemed to entertain a growing conviction that his position as Minister of Militia and Defence made him all-powerful and superior to the prime minister. For too long the prime minister seemed similarly convinced, but this was outright defiance, and when Hughes started dictating what should and should not be done, Sir Robert had had enough. He asked for and received Sir Sam's resignation. The government's prestige had suffered severely from Hughes' reign, with war-contract scandals, shoddy equipment for men fighting for their lives, and a comic-opera administration in England.

On November 23, 1916, Mr. A. E. Kemp replaced Hughes and soon a Ministry of Overseas Military Forces, headed by Sir George Perley, was created to resolve the muddle. Major-General Turner reluctantly relinquished his command of the 2nd Canadian Division to become Commander of Canadian Forces in Britain. Major-General H. E. Burstall took over the divisional command.

Winter in the front line promised to be much the same as the year before. Destruction, death, and foul weather still prevailed, but conditions in rest billets had by this time greatly improved. The burdens of the chaplains were eased by organizations such as the Salvation Army, the Knights of Columbus and the Y.M.C.A., which set up canteens in the back areas where men could buy tea or coffee and small luxuries. Here they could relax in warm bright huts, gather round a piano, forget the trenches in songs of the day or ribald parodies. Sometimes professional entertainers came from England to put on a show, but there were always plenty of volunteers willing to do a turn or clown for an appreciative audience. Female impersonators were specially popular.

There were performers of real talent in the Corps, and headquarters, soon realizing that such shows were valuable in maintaining morale, authorized concert parties to tour the rear lines; the entertainers were rewarded by getting a spell out of the trenches. The most famous of these was organized by Merton Plunkett, a Y.M.C.A. entertainment officer who, with the honorary rank of captain, joined the 3rd Division in 1916. Show business was his forte and he soon picked the likely performers. By 1917 he had a party of ten veterans, calling themselves the Dumbells, none of them above the rank of sergeant. One of them was Plunkett's young brother Al, who at eighteen had been in the army for two years. Al could impersonate a pretty girl successfully, but his most popular role was that of a dandy in a scrounged suit of formal "tails," evening cape, top hat and cane, singing "The Wild, Wild Women are making a Wild Man of Me." Sergeant Ted Charters in clerical garb had his audience helpless with laughter with a piously delivered sermon, taking as his text: "Be ye prepared, for no man knoweth when inspection cometh." But the show-stopper was a private in the 9th Field Ambulance named Ross Hamilton. With supplementary aids he could impersonate a beautiful brunette and sing falsetto. None of the "girls" in the chorus line could compete. The troupe wrote their own skits and borrowed popular songs from current musicals.

General Lipsett gave his blessing to the Dumbells, who took their name from the insignia of the 3rd Division, a red dumbbell, and they spent the rest of the war entertaining the troops. Captain Plunkett increased the number of performers, who between them had an average of sixteen months' service in the front lines; when not giving concerts they served as stretcher-bearers. Performing close behind the battle area, shell-fire sometimes broke up a show, and men in the audience at five o'clock might be back in the line and dead three hours later.

The Dumbells' show survived the war by ten years. They played at the Coliseum in London, on Broadway in New York, and toured many times across Canada playing to packed houses everywhere.

Meanwhile, on the Western Front, there were no major engagements in that winter of 1916-17, other than the French counter-offensive at Verdun. The balance sheets for the Battle of the Somme were being tallied by both sides. From some million and a quarter casualties, little had been gained outside of experience for those commanders who chose to profit from the lessons.

The Germans learned that the policy of rigidly defending a line to the last man, while heroic, was not necessarily sound. The old saying that "he who fights and runs away lives to fight another day" had merit—as long as he had some place safe to run. They therefore introduced a policy of limited flexibility in defence, and spent the winter building a safe place to run to—the Hindenburg Line.

It was built mostly by Russian prisoners of war during that fall and winter, and consisted of several lines of deep trenches and a series of forward outpost zones. Each zone had numerous strong-points, and connecting trenches—called switches—gave quick and safe passage for communications, supplies and reinforcements. The whole system was heavily fortified with concrete, wire, machine-guns and artillery. This was defence in depth, an "impregnable line" behind forward armies, and a fortified base on which to fall back in the event of severe reverses or strategic withdrawal.

The British and French had made plans in the fall of 1916 for a co-ordinated offensive in the spring, but that winter the French Commander-in-Chief, General Joffre, fell out of favour. He was replaced by General R. Nivelle, who had just achieved conspicuous success in his counter-offensive at Verdun.

Nivelle scrapped the Joffre-Haig plan, substituted one of his own, and persuaded Prime Minister Lloyd George to place the British Commander-in-Chief, General Haig, under his French authority. The outraged Haig submitted on a temporary basis only. His role was to pin down large masses of the enemy in mid-March, while Nivelle employed shock tactics on a large scale, to break through and disrupt enemy defences.

General Nivelle's security measures were lax and the Germans gained knowledge of his plans. Although aware of this, Nivelle refused to change them, and the Germans took full advantage of their information. They were seriously engaged on other fronts and were anxious to avoid, for the time being, any struggle in Western Europe. Ordered to retreat, their Second and First Armies, and wings of their Seventh and Sixth, withdrew silently and skilfully to their Hindenburg Line. Evacuating towns and villages, destroying or polluting wells, laying booby traps, blowing up or barricading highways, they laid waste an area of nearly one hundred miles between Soissons and Arras that averaged twenty miles in depth.

The Allied armies, intent on preparations for a big push, woke one morning to find there was no one to push. The enemy had eluded a pincer movement. Effective pursuit was prevented by their delaying actions and the scorched earth. This was a serious blow. Contact with the enemy was lost and it would take weeks to repair roads and rails and bring up supplies. Efforts to make Nivelle abandon his plan failed. It would merely be somewhat put back.

In the Canadian Corps, General Byng and his commanders carefully analysed the Somme battles to find the weak links and the means of strengthening them. The effectiveness of indirect machine-gun fire had been clearly demonstrated, but Brutinel, closely scrutinizing results, felt there was considerable room for improvement.

It was necessary, he decided, to broaden the outlook of some of the officers and bring them to think in terms of co-ordinated action on much larger fronts. There was a lack of boldness in the selection of emplacements for co-ordinated barrages, and for that matter, in the employment of machine-guns in general. Hard training would eradicate these imperfections.

The formation of the brigade machine-gun companies in 1915 had been an important step towards establishing machine-gunnery as a separate arm, but the Vickers guns were heavy brutes to manhandle into position, along with tripods, ammunition and belt boxes. The extraordinary bravery and spirit of self-sacrifice displayed by machine-gunners could not compensate for the evident need to perfect the organization which the weapon required, both administratively and tactically. Generally the guns had been badly employed—certainly not to their full effectiveness for all concerned.

The problem was how to organize and train the crews. Brutinel's answer to this was the formation of a corps; so in January 1917, General Byng applied for the establishment of the Canadian Machine Gun Corps. It was not authorized until after the Battle of Vimy Ridge.

At that time the entire personnel of the machine-gun service, 222 officers and 5,943 other ranks, was still on the strength of infantry units, and seniority and promotion were settled by infantry lists. In an urgent recommendation to the recently created Overseas Ministry of Canadian Forces, General Byng writes that this situation is "highly unsatisfactory and has resulted in extravagance, inefficiency and discontent. . . . As things are at present the Machine Gun Companies of the Canadian Corps must inevitably break down during active and prolonged operations."

Traditionally the machine-gun was considered a direct-fire defensive weapon to be used like a rifle, the other extreme from its early use like artillery. But Brutinel was to employ it both defensively and offensively from the beginning. He used the 1st Motors as an independent unit in support of infantry, and although his system of predicted fire was most unorthodox, he soon proved that his theory of map-shooting and harassing night fire was practical beyond any doubt. In the offence, actively supporting the infantry in attack, his guns were used not separately, but in pairs or more, each position having a fan-shaped arc of fire, soon to be used to direct a creeping protective barrage *ahead* of the infantry that would reduce casualties enormously.

It is unlikely that such revolutionary ideas of a comparatively junior officer would have been adopted in any other army, but this was a militia army. Ingenuity was encouraged, not frowned on, and Sir Julian Byng, although a Regular, had a receptive and imaginative mind. He recognized the possibilities and encouraged Brutinel to develop his ideas.

While the successful battle at Verdun was still in progress a party of British and Canadian officers studied the operation on the ground. Fighting had been severe and losses heavy, but morale was high and the French soldiers were determined to hold every inch of ground regardless of cost. Acting on what had been learned on the Somme and seen at Verdun, General Byng and his commanders started preparations for coming battles. The troops kept in training through patrols and raids. Many successful sorties netted good returns in the way of information to be of great value later. Much credit goes to the engineers and pioneers, whose courage matched their skill in demolitions and tunnelling. But in the midst of many successes, the most elaborately planned raid failed cruelly.

It was a 4th Division undertaking on the left section of Vimy Ridge and tear gas and chlorine were to be used. This meant working parties had to carry heavy cylinders by night and set them in the parapet, flexible hoses directed towards the enemy. It was terribly hard work, but all stood to in the pre-dawn of February 26, waiting for the signal.

Thirty minutes before zero hour the attack was put off—wind and weather conditions were unfavourable. For four days this procedure was repeated until strain and sleeplessness began to take their toll. On the fifth morning, March 1, all seemed well. Then, at the last minute, favourable conditions suddenly changed. Cancellation came so close to the deadline that orders failed to reach the 11th and 12th Infantry Brigades and one battery of artillery. A weak bombardment gave the signal to release the gas and go over the top.

Everything went wrong. There was ample evidence that the Germans were ready and waiting; they let go with everything they had. The gas blew back on the stationary brigade that had received the cancellation orders, and shell-fire smashed some of their gas cylinders. Small gains were made here and there, a few prisoners taken, but the line was ragged and the men, appalled by the almost complete lack of fire-support, were cut to pieces and forced to withdraw as the Germans started their counter-attack.

As dawn broke and the counter-attack petered out, the Canadians started the grisly task of counting losses. In no-man's-land lay the bodies of 687 dead and wounded, two battalion commanders among the many officers lost. It was a blow from which some battalions never recovered.

Suddenly a big Scottish sergeant of the 73rd Batallion threw down his rifle and equipment and, jumping on the parapet, waved a first-aid field dressing like a white flag.

Not a shot was fired. Instead a German N.C.O. stood up and waved his helmet. Then a couple more Germans followed suit, as did some Canadians down the line. In a few moments an unofficial truce was recognized along the whole divisional front, and practically everyone was out to bring back their wounded. The opposing troops were Bavarians, and an eye-witness relates that several seriously wounded Canadians were brought from behind enemy lines, where small gains had been relinquished.

In spite of this disaster, as the month advanced, raids became almost a nightly routine to gather up-to-the-minute information for the coming offensive. It would be known as the Arras Offensive, or Battles of Arras, and included the action at Vimy Ridge and the first, second and third battles of the Scarpe.

The Canadians were to be responsible for capturing the whole of the main crest of Vimy Ridge, considered one of the most important tactical features on the whole of the Western Front. Its capture was considered vital to the French General Staff.

In the early days, when the Germans failed to take Paris, they fell back along the Ridge, a nine-mile barrier that dominated the area with natural features advantageous to a defending force. The French had made heroic and dauntless assaults in 1915, only to be driven back with fruitless loss of life. The British had taken over the front in 1916, but with no more success in carrying the Ridge than the French—in fact they had lost ground. It was generally agreed that it was impregnable, for the Germans by 1917 had built tunnels and deep dugouts, fortifying the position with three main defensive lines, rows and rows of heavy barbed wire, and a network of concrete machine-gun nests.

Now the Canadians were to have a try at capturing it.

9

1917: THE BATTLE OF VIMY RIDGE

Crucial events made that spring of 1917 memorable. The Russian Revolution began on March 12, and although the Russian troops continued to fight for a time, disorganized and ill-equipped, they contributed little. A separate peace was signed in November. Nearly a month after the revolution, on April 6, Germany's ruthless submarine warfare brought the United States into the war. This boosted morale, but was of no practical value to those preparing for the imminent battle.

General Byng and his commanders had laid careful plans with much preliminary training and preparations. Troops rehearsed on a course taped out to simulate enemy lines, and were schooled in the use of German guns which when captured could be turned on retreating Germans. Tunnellers built subways twenty-five feet underground leading to the front lines. These provided protection for movement of troops and telephone wires. British and Canadian sappers repaired and maintained miles of roads and built new ones. Pipelines were laid and reservoirs built to supply water for men and horses. Railway troops laid miles of rail; signallers, miles of wire for communications; and tens of thousands of tons of ammunition were carried forward and stacked in dumps.

From their dominant position the enemy had full view of the roads and rails, but ingenuity on the part of the engineers overcame that disadvantage. They erected poles on either side of the roads and strung banners of hessian at calculated distances apart, like Main Street of a small town on the First of July. From a distance the pale sackcloth looked like the road, but an empty road, not worth the cost of a shell, while underneath traffic flowed undetected. Similarly, across the rail lines banners of coarse netting known as scrim were hung. Odd-coloured pieces of rag were woven into the scrim, simulating the rough ground around, while underneath rail trucks passed safely to and fro.

Critics, not all of them outside the Corps, voiced misgivings and adverse opinions about the machine-gun preparations. Senior officers, among them gunners, were unconvinced that indirect machine-gun fire was effective. The range was too limited for offensive warfare; gun crews would be unable to keep pace with the infantry; the colossal amount of ammunition needed took space and transport that could be better used for supplies to other branches. Above all, indirect fire was too risky—all ranks were unequal to the task of such specialized training.

The detractors could not have been more wrong in this last assumption. The infantry had become familiar with and grateful for machine-gun overhead fire at the Somme. Now a protective creeping barrage ahead of advancing troops was to be introduced and this increased their morale and sense of security. Men who had suffered cruel punishment after the Germans adopted indirect machine-gun fire had no doubts as to the method's effectiveness.

The criticism did not shake the faith of the top-ranking commanders and the intense training and rehearsals went on.

It was natural that the French were intensely concerned with the preparations. The Chief of the French General Staff paid a long visit to the Corps, where all details were explained in full. He was particularly interested in the machine-gun plans and requested that he be informed of the results. After he left Sir Julian sent for Brutinel, saying in effect: "You'll have to make a full report, Bruty, for the benefit of our French friends. They've taken the plans of machine-gun employment for before, during, and after the battle."

"A report from me would be of little value," replied Brutinel stiffly. "The report should be made by the Germans themselves. They, and they alone, can give first-hand information on the subject from the business end of it."

General Byng laughed and agreed. A questionnaire was prepared which the Corps Intelligence Officers would use on the prisoners as they came in. The answers to the questions would be sent to the French army without delay.

For a whole week beforehand Canadian artillery bombarded villages, demolished enemy trenches, cut supply routes. Since night firing would disclose battery positions, the machine-guns took over at nightfall and their harassing fire prevented the enemy from repairing the damage. This superb combined action was unquestionably a factor in the success of the battle.

On Easter Monday, April 9, at four a.m. the troops were in position, all warmed by a hot meal and a tot of rum. The battle opened at dawn in a driving snowstorm that made the ground almost impassable and increased the difficulties in the maze of shell-holes. The infantry attacked with their known courage and gallantry, but now with a new confidence, supported by the machine-guns and protected by the artillery. Intense fire-power was the best ally they could ask for.

In the first phase there was fierce hand-to-hand fighting, but most of the opposition came from enemy snipers and machine-gun crews in strong-points. By late afternoon the 1st, 2nd, and 3rd Divisions, at great cost, had achieved their objectives. The 4th Division, assigned to Hill 145, the highest and most important feature of that part of the Ridge, encountered strong defences and suffered heavy casualties. They were considerably later in achieving their goal, but in two days all the main part of Vimy Ridge was in their hands. There remained the northern tip, known as the Pimple, to capture.

The importance of the Pimple may be judged by the strength of the German defences; it was a maze of trenches, tunnels and deep dugouts that had withstood many Allied raids. Its capture was a combined operation by the Canadian Corps and the 1st British Corps. Fresh troops of the German 5th Guards Grenadier Regiment had been rushed up as reinforcements.

The attack at five a.m. on April 12, opened in a gale of sleet and snow, but the wind blew from the west and the Germans, both surprised and blinded by the driving sleet, were overpowered. By daylight the Canadians and the British 73rd Brigade had driven them off the Ridge. Accepting defeat, the enemy withdrew to strong positions in the plain, leaving behind guns and ammunition which the Canadian gunners used to advantage.

The ground was never again occupied by the Germans. The Canadian success had resulted in the capture of more ground, more prisoners, more guns than any previous British offensive on the Western Front. Congratulations poured in from France, Canada and Britain, with a message from His Majesty King George himself.

The achievements of the Canadians at Vimy Ridge could be described as only a minor engagement on the left of the British who were fighting a major battle, *but it was the first decisive victory for the British forces in two and a half years of war*. Moreover, it was the capture of the Ridge, hitherto considered impregnable, that permitted the Allied armies to engage the enemy without his domination from the high ground.

"The Battle of Vimy Ridge," to quote from an account in the Army Historical Section in Ottawa, "constitutes one of the most complete and decisive engagements of the war. The Germans were utterly defeated and driven from the field. No serious attempt at a counter-attack was made."

Again from the same Department, in the *History of the Machine Gun Corps*: "The success of the Vimy operation . . . marked the beginning of a new era in machine-gun work. The machine-gun methods of the Canadian Corps at once became the object of study by staff representatives and machine-gun experts from other corps of the British and French Armies. By the end of 1917 the machine-gun at last took its proper place in the instruction and practice of the British Army as a weapon intermediate between infantry and artillery."

As Colonel Brutinel suggested, the testimony of the German prisoners on the effectiveness of the machine-gun tactics was sent to the French without added comment. Summed up, it was as follows:

> By night, machine-gun fire made it difficult to repair trenches knocked down by artillery fire by day.
>
> The bringing in of supplies was hampered greatly and was practically impossible during the last few days because of the density of indirect machine-gun fire.
>
> Evacuation of the wounded was increasingly difficult and almost impossible during the last three nights before the attack.

The intense machine-gun fire made it impossible to man the parapets once the attack started.

Vimy asserted beyond all doubt the Canadians' capacity for offensive warfare. Full credit was given them by French and British headquarters. The Germans themselves rendered unwilling tribute to their courage and ability, and all branches of the Corps acquitted themselves with honour.

The establishment of the Canadian Machine Gun Corps was authorized shortly after, but the cart went before the horse, for in the battle the whole tactical employment of assembling and fighting the guns was on a corps basis.

A few weeks later the French Command requested that the Canadian Machine Gun Officer, Colonel Brutinel, be permitted to give a series of lectures on organization and employment to their own Machine-Gun School at Chalon-sur-Marne.

The school was run by Captain de Grammont Lesparre and was supervised by General M. E. Fayolle, then commanding a group of armies.

A large number of machine-gunners assembled there—one from practically every formation from brigade up to army. For the latter part of the course staff officers arrived from the Ministry of War and the Ministry of Munitions and Supply. On the night before the last lecture, Brutinel received in his hut a large delegation of officers. Knowing it was not quite ethical, they nevertheless asked him to listen to what they had to say.

Machine-guns in the French army, they said, did not lend themselves to the method of firing that had been adopted in the Canadian Corps. There were two guns; the St. Etienne, a fine weapon but most unsuitable for the stress and strain of trench work, was in plentiful supply and issued to the regiments. The other gun, the Hotchkiss, was lighter but more rugged and designed to withstand the mud and conditions of the front line, but these were retained for the communication troops while the front-line fighters had to cope with the St. Etienne. If the allocation was reversed they would be much happier, and probably better able to adopt the tactics of the Canadians.

This was a rather ticklish situation for Brutinel who was there as a guest lecturer, to teach rather than to criticize. But he was not one to shirk needful unpleasantness, and he said he would do what he could. Towards the end of that final lecture he concluded by suggesting that front-line troops would find the Hotchkiss more efficient for the purpose than the St. Etienne.

The staff officer from the War Ministry leapt to his feet. Interrupting, he said that the lecturer was overstepping the bounds of practice; the views of the Canadian officer on the use of weapons in the French army were unnecessary and unwelcome. In any case there were not sufficient Hotchkiss guns to equip the battalions.

At this General Fayolle intervened. Turning to the staff officer from the Ministry of Munitions and Supply, he asked if this was so. Could the Hotchkiss guns be produced in sufficient numbers to equip battalions?

Promptly that officer replied: "Yes, we can supply all they want. We are quite ready for it."

A heated argument broke out, and for a few moments the storm raged over the head of the visiting lecturer.

Calling for order, General Fayolle said: "This is a serious matter and should be settled by the machine-gunners themselves, not by staff officers. Whatever the theoretical aspects of the machine-gun, the men using them are more competent to say which one serves their purpose best. They must express their views. Knowing what their experience has been in these long years of fighting, I'm going to ask them to do just that. All those in favour of the St. Etienne machine-gun, stand up!"

In all that body of fighting men, only one officer stood. He happened to be sitting just in front of the officer from the War Ministry.

Then the General said: "Now all those in favour of the Hotchkiss machine-gun, stand up!"

As a body the audience rose, including the man who had stood for the St. Etienne gun.

"This seems to be rather conclusive," remarked the General. "I shall take steps to report at once to the Higher Command."

General Fayolle, however, was eager to see for himself what the machine-gun could do, and to test the safety of the overhead barrage. He asked the commandant to arrange a demonstration supporting an infantry battalion with machine-gun indirect fire.

The demonstration took place a day or so later. A battalion was deployed and supported by all the School's guns. There were no casualties, and the general was impressed.

"If you can do that, then you ought to be able to organize a surprise attack on a given point," he said. "Now in front of us we have a position—a little height overlooking the Manoir Grande—which we've taken and lost again. Without the use of artillery the surprise should be complete, so let's see what you can do by just using machine-guns."

The attack was carried out successfully, the position captured without losses, and held henceforth.

Thus was the French army convinced. Several Machine Gun Schools were organized, and the necessary handbooks written, printed and distributed within three months.

Not only the French but the Belgians, Italians and the British too, then adopted identical methods, although the organization of their machine-gun units remained somewhat different.

10

THE ROYAL CANADIAN ARTILLERY AND THE BATTLES OF ARRAS

At Vimy the honours were shared by Sir Julian Byng and the Canadians. This was the first time the Canadian divisions had fought all together as a corps with planning and preparation by their own commanders, and they had achieved great success. Born that day in their breasts was a pride in themselves and their country uninhibited by ethnic loyalties.

It had been a quick decisive victory and the victors had successfully held and consolidated their gain of 4,500 yards, on more than a four-mile front. Their casualties, 10,602, terrible as they seemed for five days, were comparatively light in the face of the enemy's great strength, and the ground was never to be lost again in that war.

It was in this battle that the artillery, in unprecedented strength, displayed the superiority it was to maintain thereafter.

Although genius was conspicuously absent on both sides in that war, there were men of brilliance and foresight. But in the British army it was well-nigh impossible to break through the crust of complacency at British G.H.Q., because the military conviction of the day was that the highest man on the ladder knew best, while those below, steadying the ladder on treacherous ice or bog, knew nothing.

General Byng, and later General Currie, differed in this respect.

Both commanders listened to men below and profited from the specialized knowledge of scientific minds, British and Canadian alike. Among these was Lieutenant-Colonel McNaughton who introduced new artillery tactics and methods that contributed largely to the increasing superiority of Canadian Corps artillery.

Andrew McNaughton was born in Saskatchewan, had studied electrical engineering at McGill University, and held a militia commission in the artillery. He was twenty-seven years old and had a Master of Science degree when war broke out. He immediately volunteered and went overseas with the 2nd Brigade, Canadian Field Artillery, in the First Contingent. By the end of the war he had won the D.S.O., been mentioned in dispatches three times, wounded twice, and promoted to brigadier general.

McNaughton's trained mind with its unique combination of science and military technology made him perfect for the artillery. Like many able soldiers, his tendency to cut through red tape sometimes got him into trouble, but as commander of the 11th Brigade, C.F.A., he had the support and encouragement of his senior commanders.

The gunnery techniques McNaughton developed in the Corps are as spectacular as those of Raymond Brutinel with the machine-guns. Difference lies in the fact that artillery has always been recognized as the dominant arm of the service, whereas the machine-gun had to be raised from a despised position of insignificance and questionable value.

By 1917 the Canadian Corps Artillery had reached an advanced state of efficiency, and this lead was maintained to the end of the war. General Currie was always eager for maximum support for the infantry and was responsible for the ultimate co-operation between the two arms that did not exist at the beginning. His posting of gunnery officers as liaison with headquarters infantry brigades did much to smooth rough spots, and increase effective operations.

At the beginning of the war the Germans had more guns and ammunition, and a far greater range. In the second Battle of Ypres in 1915, German batteries came into full view, shelling Allied men and batteries mercilessly. Not only were the Canadians' guns unable to reach them, but gunners were limited to three rounds of ammunition per gun per day. McNaughton described the situation as follows: "The infantry might point out a nest of troublesome machine-guns to the gunners, who could say: 'Sorry, we've used our quota for the day.'

"The bitter retort: 'What are you doing in the Great War anyway?' didn't contribute to co-operation."

The gunners had their troubles too. There was no standardization of ammunition. Many different kinds of shells would be sent up, all in the same consignment, varying not only in range but in conditions under which they could be used, such as the degree of moisture, velocity and wind direction. Even as late as 1918, lack of standardization was still one of the most serious limiting factors. Too often the type of shell available was wrong for the job, as in the action at Regina Trench in 1916, when field-gun shrapnel was used to cut wire.

The function of artillery is to crush out of existence a wide section of the enemy's defensive system, and to assist to the maximum the man in the front line—the infantry. Towards this objective Colonel McNaughton brought his scientific knowledge into developing unprecedented methods of artillery tactics, particularly in counter-battery work.

The position of enemy guns had to be known before they could be destroyed. Destruction must be fast and leave little time for retaliation. To this end, artillery intelligence was of primary importance. It was obtained in various ways—from aerial photography, patrols, secret agents, prisoners, intercepted wireless and, for instant action, from aerial observation relayed by wireless or dropped messages. The Canadian Signal Corps did an excellent job here as elsewhere.

Limiting factors in battles were the degree of observation and intelligence available, the quality, quantity and transport of ammunition from the railhead, and the life of the guns, for the wear and tear was high on both guns and personnel.

The enemy, of course, used similar methods and experienced like limitations, except that right up to November 1918 they had superiority in quality and design of guns. By then the British had superiority in quantity, organization and tactical employment, and these last two were largely the product of McNaughton's ability.

Flash-spotting was one development of his counter-battery operations. Placed at selected points over an area were posts manned by "spotters," equipped with survey instruments and telephones to one central station. When a spotter at one post located a hostile firing battery, the bearing was reported to the central station by a light on a switchboard. Not until all spotters registered the same location—all

Shell-burst beside crews of the Canadian Machine Gun Corps, Flanders 1917.

(Below) Auto trucks on the way to the Front.

Photo: The Public Archives of Canada.

(Right) Canadian Corps Tramway men reading a salvage notice board, May 1918.

Photo: The Public Archives of Canada.

(Far right) An Armoured car of the 1st Canadian Motor Machine Gun Brigade.

National Defence photo.

57921
BRI

(Above) Vimy Ridge, June 1917. Canadian troops making good use of a shell hole before an attack on the German trenches at night.

Photo: The Public Archives of Canada.

(Top right) General Sir Arthur Currie, G.C.M.G., K.C.B., Canadian Corps Commander, 1917-1919.

(Bottom right) Brigadier General Raymond Brutinel, C.B., C.M.G., D.S.O., Commander Canadian Machine Gun Corps, 1914-1919.

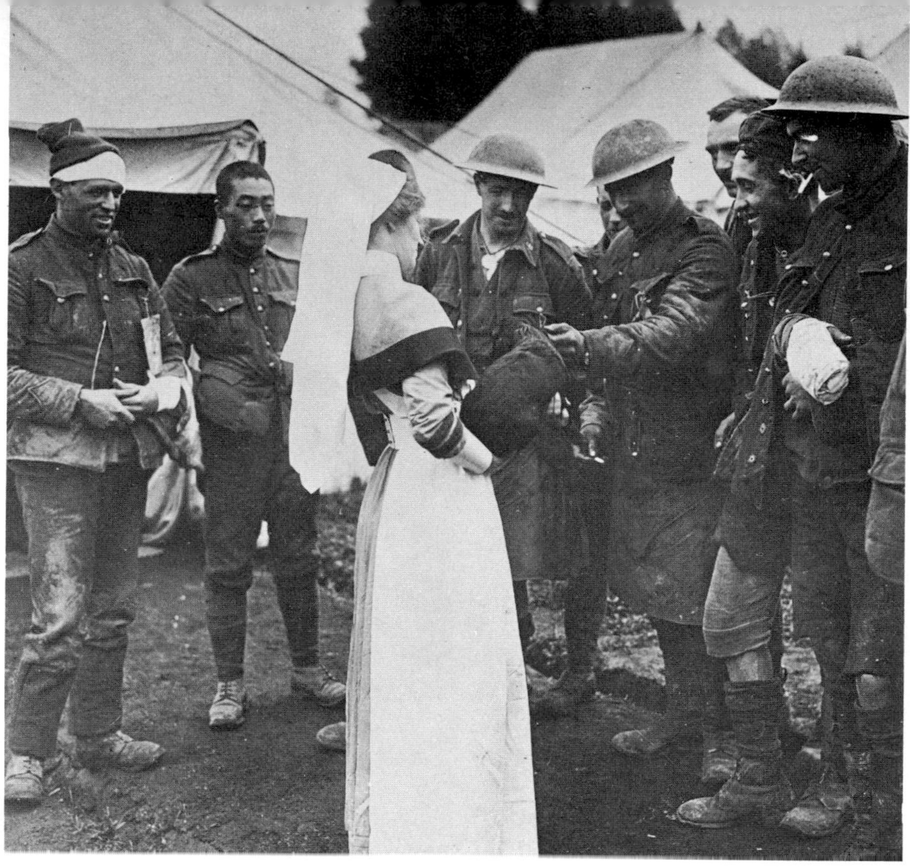

(Above) Casualty Clearing Station, October 1916. Wounded Canadian soldiers presenting a nurse with a dog brought out of the trenches.

Photo: The Public Archives of Canada.

(Top right) One of three murals painted by the Germans on the wall of a barn at Lewarde, captured by Canadian troops in 1918.

Photo: The Public Archives of Canada.

(Bottom right) The advance east of Arras, September 1918. The Canal du Nord showing construction work by Canadian troops preparatory to their crossing with supports and supplies.

Photo: The Public Archives of Canada.

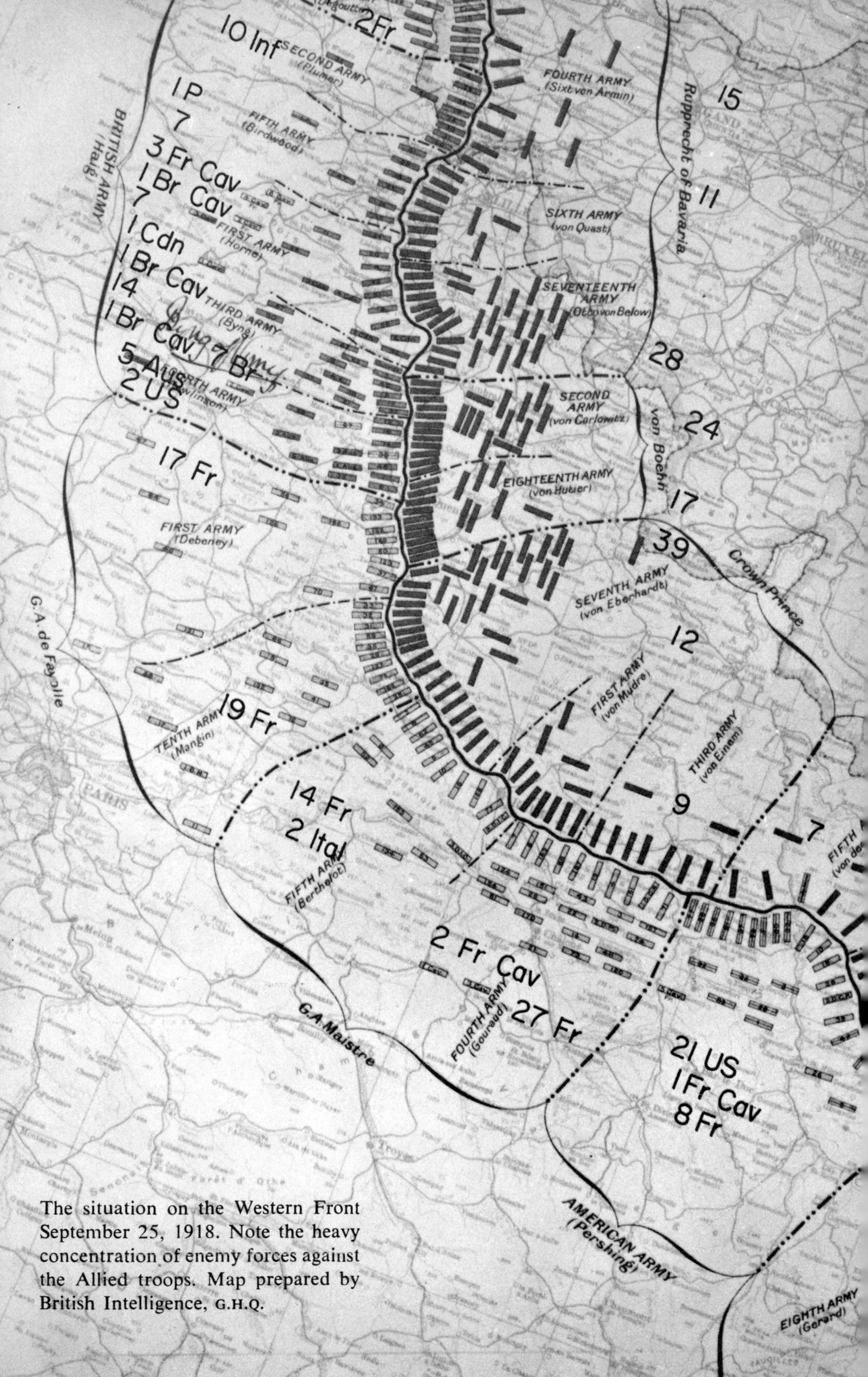

The situation on the Western Front September 25, 1918. Note the heavy concentration of enemy forces against the Allied troops. Map prepared by British Intelligence, G.H.Q.

lights flashing—was the location considered certain. The position was then plotted for the battery to aim.

Another means of location was the use of a series of microphones to record the sound waves of enemy fire, thus revealing the position of the guns. These inventions made possible the rapid destruction of German batteries, thus saving lives and defences, and marking a definite advance in military technology.

In protective barrages for infantry in attack, the Canadian gunners developed a high degree of skill. The object, of course, was to demoralize the enemy, preventing their use of rifles and machine-guns, and to screen the advance of the infantry by a wall of bursting shells and dust. But bursting shells had to be up to two hundred yards in front of the attackers, so a high degree of accuracy was vital. Artillery officers required technical skill. Time was a factor in getting trained personnel, but Colonel McNaughton worked out simplified systems of range tables and specifications that gunners could use quickly, thereby greatly increasing accuracy and reducing the time for calculation.

After the war, Major-General McNaughton paid this tribute to his commanders and his men:

I know of no other organization in the history of the war which was able to produce such a high ratio in shells to troops, nor any in which the price paid for victory was lower in personnel. This was only possible because of our leaders.

Canadians took naturally to gunnery . . . all ranks developing extraordinary skill, efficiency and dependability, and if there was ever a particularly difficult or dangerous task to do, a Canadian battery was called on to do it. Only on one occasion (Sanctuary Wood) were any guns of the Canadian Corps Artillery in German hands. All ammunition was gone and the gunners dead or wounded. The guns were recovered shortly in subsequent fighting.

After the Battle of Vimy Ridge the commanders scrutinized the action for lessons to be learned, and found them in the adverse road conditions which prevented the bringing forward of guns to advance with the infantry. For future battles, road-making was to be vigorously pressed. But success had brought an overall feeling of self-confidence to Canadians, and a sure sweet whiff of victory was in the air—small, but a change from the sour smell of frustration they had known at the Somme.

Meanwhile, Haig's offensive, of which Vimy was only a part,

started on the same day, April 9, and was intended as support for General Nivelle's campaign. But the French attack, suffering from an over-confident commander and poor security, got off to a late start and petered out with enormous casualties. As a result, Nivelle was dispatched to North Africa and replaced by Pétain.

The British Battles of Arras took place over a period of four weeks, starting with the first Battle of the Scarpe. This battle resulted in gains for the British but had unfortunate repercussions. The Fifth Army under Gough made a futile attempt to break through a strongly defended section of the Hindenburg Line at Bullecourt, using the 4th Australian Division in conjuction with eleven tanks. The decision was made the night before and launched at 4:30 a.m. There was no preliminary bombardment. The tanks led the way; several were knocked out by hostile artillery, the rest tore through barbed wire and escorted the Australians into the Hindenburg Line. In the German counter-attack that followed, the Australians were cut to pieces and some tanks captured.

The employment of the tanks was harshly criticized by officers of the Heavy Branch. Says Fuller; "The plan was hastily devised, shockingly prepared and carried out in an unco-ordinated way."

A bitter quarrel between the Australians and the Heavy Branch resulted which was not to be resolved for over a year. Tank men, experts in their own line, believed that had the available sixty tanks been used, and the attack properly prepared, they could have made a complete breakthrough, but Bullecourt remained an ugly word in Australian hearts for many months.

This first Scarpe Battle ended on April 14, and the second opened two weeks later. Canada's role was to capture the Arleux Loop, an enemy-held bulge between two salients formed by British successes in the first Scarpe Battle. This time, the British first made gains, then were repulsed. The Canadian attack succeeded, and by afternoon of the same day the Germans cancelled further counter-attacks and withdrew. The small bulge of the Arleux Loop had been reversed.

The third Scarpe Battle took place on May 3 and 4. Here the Canadians were ordered to capture the village of Fresnoy. Alerted by the loss of Arleux, the Germans were determined to make it tough for the Canadians, but the Corps Commander ensured that the same meticulous preparations were made as before. Troops rehearsed on taped trenches, simulating the enemy position; heavy guns prepared for generous fire support. As expected, they met strong opposition and suffered many casualties, but by the end of the day they occupied the objective. The enemy made several determined counter-attacks, but the Canadians held on.

Elsewhere the situation was not good. Haig's attack failed, although the Australians captured Bullecourt (*presumably* without tanks). The British official historian writes that the capture of Fresnoy by the Canadians was "the relieving feature of a day which many who witnessed it, considered the blackest of the war"; an overstatement surely. But by their own accounts, the German losses for May 3 were heaviest at Fresnoy, a position of major importance because of a long spur that gave a commanding view of German defences.

On May 5, the 1st Division went into reserve and the British took over Fresnoy. But it was too important for the Germans to relinquish without further effort. Bringing everything they had to bear, they practically wiped out the battalion holding the village and drove back the British front, including the line to the north held by the 2nd Canadian Division. The loss of such an advantageous position was a serious blow to British hopes and morale.

This battle ended the Arras offensive except for local actions. The Canadians remained in the Arras-Lens sector, the 4th Division employed in raid-like attacks to capture fortified positions between the town of Avion and the city of Lens. Limited successes were achieved, but early in June a not so successful attack was made, in which gains were made, lost, and recovered again. But with a shortage of supporting guns, the Canadians were subjected to a heavy concentration of German fire.

General Currie suggested to the First Army Commander, General Horne, that instead of trying to hold captured ground, large-scale raids—surprising, attacking, withdrawing—would be just as destructive and demoralizing to the Germans, and far less costly. General Horne concurred and these raids not only served the purpose effectively, but received credit for diverting attention from the preparations for the Second British Army's assault on Messines on June 7. This was a British victory, comparable with that of the Canadians at Vimy Ridge on which it was modelled, but on a much larger scale.

The end of June brought another sweep forward by the British 1st Corps and the Canadian Corps on the village of Avion. After a torrential rainstorm, the Souchez River to the north was flooded. Thunder and lightning of the elements mingled with that of the big guns. Over slimy, slippery ground the troops forced their way into the town, fighting hand-to-hand and house-to-house battles. They secured most of the village and consolidated gains towards the encirclement of Lens. This was a step forward in the long siege which preceded the powerful Canadian attack on Hill 70, and the partial capture of the city some weeks later.

Meanwhile something of more immediate concern to the Canadian Corps had taken place. On June 7, Lieutenant-General Sir Julian Byng was ordered to take command of the British Third Army. The Corps was to have a new commander, Arthur William Currie.

11

SIR ARTHUR CURRIE, CORPS COMMANDER

In the King's birthday honours of June 3, 1917, Arthur Currie was made a Knight Commander of St. Michael and St. George. On the 7th, Lieutenant-General Byng received his new command, and Sir Douglas Haig ordered Currie to take command of the Canadian Corps, notifying the War Office of his instructions. It was a sure way to jeopardize Currie's succession.

From the first days of the war, Canada had been resisting British domination of her overseas forces, to the bewilderment of the War Office. In all justice, colonial troops in previous wars had been administered by Imperial authorities, with the status of British regulars, as were the Australian and New Zealand contingents at this time. The War Office could not understand what the fuss was about. The Canadian government, however, insisted on retaining control over her own force in all matters except military operations in the field. Much of the credit for this belongs to Sir Sam Hughes. In the summer of 1917, the Australians finally achieved their own Corps, but up to that time they fought piecemeal where the British decreed.

Haig's brief message to the War Office, without consulting or even notifying the Canadian Overseas Minister, was aggravating in the extreme. Fortunately Sir George Perley had already recommended

Currie's promotion to Corps Commander along with equal rank for General Turner, General Officer Commanding Canadians in England. When Haig's military secretary explained that the word "temporary" had been inadvertently omitted from the order, ruffled feathers were smoothed.

Arthur Currie—an Irish Canadian—was born in Napperton, Western Ontario, in 1875. While still in his teens he went to British Columbia and there taught school before going into business in Victoria. For a time he did well, but speculations in real estate left him in serious financial difficulties when the land boom petered out, just before the war.

Years before he had joined the Militia, advancing rapidly and earning his commission and the regard of an Imperial officer, Major L. J. Lipsett, one of those posted to Canada to instruct the growing Canadian army. Evidence of Currie's leadership qualities came early, for in the officers' mess he was usually at the bottom of any devilry, leading his fellow-officers in pranks and practical jokes that were rarely appreciated by his C.O. Responsibility and the war sobered him, but contrary to widespread belief, Currie had a good sense of fun and his irony was too often interpreted literally.

In 1914 he was thirty-eight when Sam Hughes called him for command of the 2nd Infantry Brigade, where he soon inspired the confidence and respect of his men. From the first days in action, they knew him as a senior officer who stayed close to the front lines—chanced shot and shell to see conditions for himself and make his own reconnaissance. This was a practice he continued later as Corps Commander.

Before the Second Battle of Ypres, Currie had no course but to rely on his peacetime militia training for waging war, but with a natural flair for command he learned much from two years' battle experience under able commanders like Alderson, Byng, and British army generals Allenby, Plumer, and Horne. He soon gained their professional respect, but from 1915 on, a clique of his own countrymen in England and Canada came to regard him with growing enmity.

Shortly after the Ypres battle Currie presided over a board of inquiry on the Ross rifle. The verdict was a damning condemnation of the weapon, and this infuriated Hughes. He refused to believe that in rapid fire the moving parts seized, making it worse than useless, and impelling men to fling it over the parapet in frustrated fury—retrieving it after dark because it had to be accounted for.

When Sir John French, on the strength of the Board's report, ordered the Ross withdrawn and Lee-Enfields issued to the 1st Division, Hughes blamed Currie—not without reason.

Politically Currie was a Liberal, but his country came first and he was scrupulously loyal to the government. He never asked favours, never yielded to political pressure, but was more vehement than diplomatic about expressing his opinions. He was also not beyond directly approaching the Prime Minister over the heads of senior officials if he believed it sufficiently urgent, and naturally this was resented.

When promoted to command the 1st Division in the fall of 1915, Currie openly opposed the appointment of the Minister's son as commander of the 1st Infantry Brigade. There was no personal animosity, the two were good friends. Currie simply did not consider Garnet Hughes sufficiently competent to command a brigade and did not want him in his division in that capacity. This did not increase his popularity with the Minister, who saw to it that his son received the appointment anyway.

Before the end of the winter of 1915-16 Hughes and Currie tangled again. This time it concerned the Minister's efforts to make the Corps a "national" force, replacing British staff officers with Canadians. Max Aitken supported Hughes, but in Canada R. B. Bennett, parliamentary secretary to the Prime Minister, accused Aitken of stirring up trouble by influencing Sir Robert into thinking the War Office had a scheme to supersede Canadians in senior posts.

Currie, who seemed to have a lot to say as a divisional commander, would have none of it, and bluntly expressed his views.

"In my opinion," he wrote, "no Imperial in this division could at present be replaced by a Canadian officer now serving and available, without great loss of efficiency. It is not a question of whether a man is a Canadian or otherwise. It is one of the best man for the job. Sentiment must not sway our better judgment."

As the war progressed the old, sad problem of reinforcements became more pressing. Canada was a country of something over seven million people, yet the Militia Department seemed to think her manpower unlimited and promised a force of 500,000 volunteers, aiming at a total of six divisions. Early in the war, in an exuberant speech in Toronto, Hughes had even declared his intention of raising twenty-one, which nobody took seriously. But under pressure from Hughes and the Chief of Imperial General Staff, a fifth division began to assemble in England in the fall of 1916.

Battles like the Somme, with its 24,000 Canadian casualties, were bound to thin the ranks of the Corps in France. Hence, battalions arriving in England allocated to the new division were instead broken up and the men sent to France as reinforcements, the commanding officers reverting to considerably lower rank or banished to Canadian depots in the Shorncliffe area where they were known as Shorncliffe Colonels. There on full pay, they idled in frustration.

Although Byng was Corps Commander, for some reason Currie was blamed for this situation and individual feeling began to build up against him in England and Canada that spread like a ground fire. Fortunately the cabinet had grasped the significance of the huge casualty lists and, knowing the impossibility of reinforcing more divisions in the field, withheld approval for a fifth. Finally a compromise was reached with the War Office by permitting the mobilization of a division for home defence in the United Kingdom. Garnet Hughes was promoted to major-general and given command in February 1917. Actually the division did serve as a reinforcement pool and its manpower was gradually absorbed by the Corps. One year later, what was left of the division was disbanded and the remaining men went to war.

Although Sir Sam Hughes had by this time left the cabinet, his animosity towards Currie had become almost a mania and his influence was still strong and far reaching. He never ceased denouncing him, and in the short period between Currie taking "temporary" command of the Corps and confirmation of the appointment, the undercurrent of opposition surged to the top in rumours that influential Canadians were working behind the scenes with their own ideas as to the policies of the Corps and their own nominee for command.

Two days after Currie took over as acting commander the Canadian representative at G.H.Q. called on him. Currie records, "he wanted to suggest a dicker . . . but I would not accept any position with strings on it." Days later in London, hearing that Garnet was angling for command of the 1st Division, Currie made it clear that he would not accept General Garnet Hughes as a divisional commander in his Corps. Garnet called on him in his London hotel.

Up to that time the two men had remained friends in spite of the former Minister's enmity. To do Garnet justice he could not believe that Currie would obstruct his promotion. Other commanders, far more senior and important than Currie, used their seniority to surround themselves with their friends, and loyally defended and protected such friends, though they showed themselves less than competent. Haig set the example in his retention of Gough, who too many times failed the Fifth Army, and of Charteris, who, if the historians are correct, conjured optimistic reports from pessimistic intelligence for his commander-in-chief, with disastrous results to the British armies.

Garnet only saw Currie's decision as a rebuff. It was incomprehensible to him that the Commander believed the lives of his men and the cause were at stake; the need for able leaders imperative. Currie, embarrassed at having to reject his friend, was probably blunt and clumsy in putting across his point of view. The stormy three-hour meeting ended a good friendship.

More trouble was brewing. Of that month Sir Arthur wrote: "I am importuned, coaxed, threatened, and they sought to bribe me. I was told that General Hughes would have to get the 1st Division; that there was a combination in England and in Canada for him that neither I nor any other man could beat; that his father wanted him to get the position and that God help the man who fell out with his father."

Currie had already fallen out with "father," and when he appointed Brigadier General A.C. Macdonell commander of the 1st Division the threats began to materialize. It was a sinister, nebulous campaign, never to come out in the open, but Currie's diary, his correspondence and later events point unerringly to its existence.

Who besides Hughes were instigators, is still a matter for conjecture. Currie's biographer, Colonel Urquhart, believed Aitken to be involved. A Canadian from New Brunswick, Aitken had lived in England for some years, and was a member of Parliament in the Bonar Law government. A newspaper magnate, in the space of five years he was knighted, created a baronet, and in 1917 raised to the peerage as Lord Beaverbrook of Beaverbrook, New Brunswick. A close friend of Sam Hughes, he certainly had a long finger in the Canadian military pie.

Whoever the instigators, there was a very real and very powerful cabal who from that time on relentlessly did all they could to remove Currie. In July, without previous warning, his creditors in Canada suddenly demanded settlement of all debts, threatening legal proceedings if not met immediately. Currie had only his pay, nothing more. In the midst of taking over a major command at a critical period of the war, the Corps Commander was faced with bankruptcy and the end of his career.

The Overseas Minister, Sir George Perley, through whom much of the correspondence passed, was deeply troubled and suggested that Ottawa cope with the problem. The Minister of Militia and Defence, the Honorable Sir Edward Kemp, recommended to the Privy Council that the debts be settled by the Department and repaid by Sir Arthur when he could do so. Perley and Kemp realized that this was not merely vital to Currie, but a matter of life and death to the Corps as it then existed, and at that time fighting one of its toughest battles at Lens and Hill 70. But the members of the Privy Council could not make a decision. They directed that the matter stand over for three months.

This delay could have sealed Currie's fate had it not been for the generosity of two brother officers who met his obligations, and whom Sir Arthur later repaid in full.

For the present his personal problems were solved, but the Corps Commander's most difficult task remained—that of dealing with Canadian Headquarters in London, a nest of intrigue and hostility. The intervention of Sir George Perley helped to some degree, but back in Canada a federal election, based on the Military Service Act, was to be held in December and candidates in electioneering speeches circulated lies and abuse about Sir Arthur.

Reports appeared in Canadian papers to the effect that Currie was in ill-health; that he had applied for a much-needed furlough; that he did not get on well with the British commanders. These reports appeared in England in Beaverbrook's paper *Canadian Daily Record*, and when Currie took him to task, writing that "the Canadian reports are unfounded propaganda on somebody's part," the Beaver replied denying that the rumour originated in his paper—that it came from a news cable from the Militia Department in Ottawa. Bitterly Currie remarked to Garnet Hughes that the publisher of the *Canadian Daily Record* was "sufficiently au fait with facts so there was no need to republish the story."

Among the Currie Papers in the Dominion Archives in Ottawa are many personal letters written after Currie became Corps Commander which combine congratulations with warnings. From Canada a friend writes, "There is a movement afloat to get rid of Currie", and links the name of General Sir R. E. W. Turner with that of Sir Sam Hughes, also a letter from Tom W. James of the Great War Veterans Association states: "Grieved and hurt by unjust propaganda launched against you from time to time by this underhand force. As a whole the boys are right with you." The one-time Corps Commander General Sir E. A. H. Alderson sent his congratulations, adding: "I had a fear it might be otherwise"; while Major-General Sir Sam Steele, the mountie-turned-soldier commander of the Shorncliffe area, spoke out more plainly. An excerpt from a long letter leaves no doubts of his concern.

Dated January 6, 1918, General Steele writes that he regrets not having seen Currie in London and goes on to say:

This would have been much better talked over than written in this way, but as you need fear nobody, here goes.

A mutual friend of ours who is a man of wealth here and in Canada told me there is an intrigue working against you and I believe him. You will no doubt remember that during the first week of June last, I saw and congratulated you later on regarding your prospects for the command of the Corps. Well at that time, another who was in England was trying hard to get it, although unless I am much mistaken, he is unfitted for it. The men helping had given themselves away to me, little knowing that I had said to you that I hoped you would get it. They had tried hard to get Sir Douglas Haig, one of them told me, to put an alternative name with yours in the hopes that their man would be the other, and your chances would have been lost, but Sir Douglas would not bite. He stated, I was informed, that if he put in an alternative name it would be a British army and not a Canadian army man. This did not prevent them from showering cables to Ottawa for their man, in vain, I am glad to say, for it would have been the ruin of the Corps, as it had been of the 2nd Division, if he had been appointed. It [the 2nd Division] had been as fine a body of men . . . as any I have ever seen. It was nearly ruined, but has since done well—but in that man's time it was a failure, as everything else has been since.

Now what is on hand is for that man to get the Corps as soon as they can turn you out, and give the Canadians in England to a man who has never been a soldier, but is a shrewd, strong and tricky person. This is the yarn and I believe it. You must trust no one.

There is a recent brigadier in France who was with the gang to get the Corps for your rival, so be careful—he may be in on this. I can be a strong friend and can help, although I am sure you cannot be disturbed. You have done well and you can trust me.

In a second letter, following closely on the first, General Steele warns: "Don't go home. Your enemies will keep you there!"

Answering both letters on January 9, Sir Arthur thanks General Steele and adds: "I know a great deal about the cables to Ottawa and I know that the recommendation for my appointment to the Corps was opposed right up to the doors of the Privy Council."

But in Canada just before the December election, the Canadian press reported, "General Currie has been relieved of his command for inefficiency exhibited in the last battle (Passchendaele) and excessive loss of life." This was attributed to the campaigning Liberals, among them Frank Oliver, member of Parliament for Edmonton. But when the respected Sir Wilfrid Laurier used this spurious report in a political speech on December 5, 1917, Currie felt indeed betrayed.

A few days later a telegram, jointly signed by editors of several Canadian newspapers, arrived at Corps Headquarters addressed to "General Sir Arthur Currie, or to the Acting Commander of the Canadian Corps." Currie at once wrote Sir George Perley demanding official denial of the press report. He added that for the action at Passchendaele he was honoured by the French and Belgians—knifed in the back by Canadians.

"I have played the game with everyone from start to finish and have a right to expect it will be played with me."

Perley cabled the Prime Minister and the report was denied, but the seeds of doubt and suspicion were already sown in the minds of Canadians at home, which later matured into the ugly weeds of vilification and slander.

It was a whispering campaign started by no one quite knew whom, as is the case with such campaigns, but it was conducted with a deadly efficiency that could have undermined the Corps, and did poison the minds of Canadians who should have known better.

As Currie's stature grew in the eyes of Allied commanders at the front it shrank in the minds of the non-combatants at home. Gradually the poison did seep into the Corps, through reinforcements and letters from home. It could have destroyed the force, except that harmony on the staffs at every level of Currie's command was unique, and for the most part the fighting men remained loyal and devoted—a common bond that made of the Corps a single entity and saved it from disintegration.

This slanderous campaign continued long after the war was over. In the House of Commons, where there is no redress, Sir Sam Hughes on several occasions made statements accusing Currie of cowardice, deliberate slaughter of men for his own aggrandizement, incompetence, that he never went within range of shells, and that "you cannot find one soldier returning from France who will not curse the name of the officer who ordered the attack on Mons." It is all in Hansard, a verbatim record of speeches made in the House.

There were members of Parliament—Brigadier General W. A. Griesbach of Edmonton, Richard Clive Cooper of Vancouver, Colonel Cyrus W. Peck, V.C., of Skeena, all of whom had served with Currie in the Corps—who hotly defended their commander and took Hughes to task for his lies. But the saboteurs had done their work well and the impression remained in spite of leading editorials in papers like that in the Toronto *Globe* early in March 1919.

"The terrors of war," said the *Globe*, "have been great and manifold for our gallant men in France, but Sir Sam Hughes is a greater [terror] than any of them. The enemy never dealt a fouler blow than that directed by Sir Sam Hughes against the leaders of the Canadian Army still in the field and unable to defend themselves."

General Currie was reassured privately by individual members of the cabinet that the government would support and defend him, but the time never seemed quite ripe. In spite of pressure from the opposition and returned officers on the government side, no action was taken, no public declaration of confidence. The Prime Minister, when appealed to, privately gave lip service to Currie's great qualities and services, but he never confirmed them openly. Had the government emphatically and collectively denied them, the rumours might have been killed and the rumour-mongers discredited.

There is every evidence of the cabinet's confidence in Sir Arthur. Why then, did it remain silent?

12

HILL 70 AND PASSCHENDAELE

Normally the centre of France's coal-mining industry, the city of Lens had been occupied since 1914 in spite of subsequent British attacks. By the summer of 1917, it was a battered shell-torn ruin, heavily fortified nevertheless, by a cross-work of trenches with communication and support lines, deep dugouts and strong-points—a so-called impregnable position.

In July the capture of the city was assigned to the Canadians. It was Currie's first tactical task as Corps Commander, and he took himself to a height of land to study and survey the position.

To the north the city was dominated by a prominence known as Hill 70, on the slopes of which were built-up suburbs. Currie considered this hill to be far more tactically important than the city, and he persuaded General Horne to make this the initial Canadian objective. The capture of Lens could wait.

The weather was so bad that the attack on Hill 70 was postponed to mid-August. In the intervening time the Canadians made hit-and-run raids on the Germans with demoralizing effect. Enemy retaliation did little damage, for the raiders, leaving only outposts, usually withdrew. Sometimes a raiding party detected enemy raiders bent on a like sortie. This was real sport. A runner went back to warn the

Canadian line and the rest stalked and trapped the Germans, capturing all they did not kill. It was cowboys and Indians in deadly earnest.

The attack on Hill 70 commenced at dawn on August 15, 1917, and was no surprise to the enemy. But there was a preponderance of artillery support, supplemented by a concentration of machine-guns, for Currie was practising what he preached—fire-power in lieu of manpower.

The mobile machine-guns played a great part here, for the Canadian Machine Gun Corps was now an established arm of the service, with Brutinel in command. Also doing their part were special companies of Engineers who fired drums of burning oil into the Lens suburbs, where ruined buildings provided ideal cover for German defences. The artillery used gas shells liberally.

The Germans retaliated with shells of mustard gas from which the Canadians had suffered earlier in July. This gas blistered any exposed skin, could seriously damage eyes and lungs and was particularly insidious because its action was delayed; when it contaminated clothing and equipment it could be particularly dangerous.

Fighting was heavy, but advancing under cover of a superb protective barrage by the artillery, the Canadians achieved their early objectives, penetrating one mile on a two-mile front, capturing Hill 70 as well as some suburbs on the slope. The Germans launched furious counter-attacks but the line held. By August 18 the Canadians were secure in their gains.

In his personal diary, General Currie calls the three days' fighting "the hardest battle in which the Corps has participated" and "G.H.Q. regard it as one of the finest performances of the war." Four Victoria Crosses were awarded, three posthumously. Losses of course were high: 5,800 casualties, but only 41 Canadians taken prisoner.

As the war progressed every succeeding battle was the hardest. The Canadians had learned with every battle, and while their courage and determination had never been lacking, they had by this time acquired the experience and skill of seasoned campaigners. Their top leaders were now shrewd and gifted strategists, but other ranks, too, had absorbed much tactical know-how. Every man in a company was briefed in the plan of attack and the intentions of the commanding officer; thus if all officers were killed or wounded, non-commissioned officers, and even private soldiers could assume leadership and press the action.

Consequently, as it grew in skill and reputation, the commitments and tasks assigned the Corps became more and more difficult. "A captured German officer told a Canadian war correspondent at Hill 70 that only Von Kluck's men in 1914 had soldiers as brave and as thoroughly trained as the Canadians."

Five days later the attack on Lens proper began. The enemy, strengthened by fresh reserves, resisted fiercely. Counter-attack followed attack for three terrible days. Pit-heads and underground tunnels were crammed with Germans, steadily replacing casualties in an unending stream. A company of the 44th Battalion (Canadian), fighting on a huge heap of mine refuse known as the Green Crassier, was wiped out after firing its entire stock of bombs and ammunition. Gains and losses occurred all along the line, but the Germans were determined to hold Lens at all cost, and the cost for the Allies was too high. With insufficient resources, General Horne ordered the action broken off. For the next few weeks the front remained relatively quiet; then, at the end of September, the Canadians were relieved.

The capture of Hill 70 and parts of the city were of significant value to the Allies. The ground remained in Allied hands and the siege of Lens was maintained, but the Germans did not relinquish the rest of the city till the retreat a year later—the beginning of the end.

Early in October the Corps withdrew from General Horne's First Army and headed north. It had been generally assumed that they would be placed under the command of their former commander Sir Julian Byng, now G.O.C. Third Army, to take part in a surprise attack on Cambrai. Precedence, however, was given to the capture of Passchendaele in Flanders, in the Ypres area where the British, including Australian and New Zealand troops, had been fighting bitterly but to little effect, for two months.

The object of this northern offensive was to break through and capture the Belgian ports of Zeebrugge and Ostend, and was the brainchild of Sir Douglas Haig. Prime Minister Lloyd George and General Pétain had both expressed grave doubts of its wisdom, and Sir Henry Wilson, British liaison officer with the French Headquarters, noted in his diary, that Foch asked him who it was who wanted Haig to go on "a duck's march through the inundations to Ostend and Zeebrugge."

It would appear that Haig was abetted by Admiral Jellicoe who, alarmed at the mounting losses at sea, declared at a special meeting in June, that "Britain must either capture Zeebrugge before the end of the year or accept defeat."

Losses at sea had indeed been appalling, but Lord Jellicoe's contention that the capture of Zeebrugge and Ostend would solve the problem was unrealistic. Such losses might inconvenience the enemy, but there were German ports out of which their submarines could operate.

The Admiralty's opposition to using the convoy system seemed stubborn stupidity, although Correlli Barnett, in his book *The Swordbearers*, throws a different light on the subject. Barnett reveals that the Grand Fleet of 1914 was inferior in design and armament, and with so many mechanical breakdowns as to make it seriously undependable. The Fleet was superior only in number and reputation. Fortunately the myth of invulnerability persisted, and the German High Seas Fleet never seriously challenged it. Instead they used submarines against merchant vessels.

It is possible, therefore, that some of Lord Jellicoe's reluctance to employ the convoy system stemmed more from a lack of confidence in the Royal Navy than in the Merchant Navy, as has been inferred. Whatever the reason, Lloyd George, in July 1917, over-rode the Admiralty and ordered "peremptory action." The convoy system was introduced immediately and from that time losses at sea were greatly reduced.

Nevertheless, it seems that Jellicoe's opinions sustained the Commander-in-Chief's long-cherished obsession to capture the Belgian ports. His scheme, following the breakthrough at Passchendaele, included an amphibious landing between Ostend and Nieuport, using enormous pontoons somehow pushed or pulled across the Channel loaded with men, tanks, guns, ambulances, wagons—all the equipment for aggressive invasion.

The tanks were to land first, storm the sea-wall, slippery with seaweed, surmount a projecting coping, and then be used as power stations to haul up the rest of the cargo. How the tanks were to manoeuvre in flooded land, criss-crossed with dykes, was left to the ingenuity of the tank men and the miracles of Providence.

This plan of Haig's indicates his ignorance of tactical handling of tanks, and the conditions under which they could be used. Twenty-five years later at Dieppe, a similar but less ambitious plan failed, owing, many believe, to senior planners who lacked similar understanding of conditions and capabilities of modern weapons. As it turned out in 1917, Haig's abortive scheme cost time, money, and effort, but no lives. It was abandoned with the failure of the Passchendaele offensive.

Haig's obsession with the northern offensive was long-standing and, in spite of delayed and reluctant acquiescence of the Prime Minister and his advisers, he proceeded with his plans for the summer of 1917. Earlier the French had agreed to participate in return for Haig's support of the Nivelle fiasco, but in May serious mutinies broke out in the French army and General Pétain advised Haig that he could not promise support, either as soon or in as much strength as he had expected. Nothing daunted, Sir Douglas went ahead with his plans.

Originally the operation was to be in the hands of Generals Rawlinson of the Fourth Army, and Plumer of the Second, but late in April, Sir Douglas, for reasons of his own, replaced Rawlinson and his Fourth Army with General Gough and the Fifth. Gough did not know the land as did Rawlinson, and valuable time elapsed while he studied it.

The first step in the campaign was the attack on Messines on June 7 which was a decisive victory. General Plumer was in a position to exploit this success, but General Gough, for reasons of *his* own advised against it, and Haig listened to Gough. Delay followed delay as Gough prepared for battle and the Germans did likewise, fully alerted by the prolonged two-week bombardment in July.

The attack began on July 31. The weather was poor. The Germans were strongly entrenched and British casualties in the first four weeks numbered 68,000. By September 20, objectives for the opening day remained uncaptured. Two weeks later rain had reduced the ground to a porridge and the two army commanders advised closing down the campaign. Instead, the Commander-in-Chief ordered in the Canadians.

If hearts sank as the Canadians turned their faces towards the Ypres Salient, it is not to be wondered at. So aptly named Graveyard of an Empire, the morass of mud and blood had gulped the bodies of men from overseas dominions, Australia, New Zealand, South Africa, India, Canada, and the flower of Britain's professional army, the "Old Contemptibles"—the men of that heroic stand in 1914.

On October 2, General Haig ordered the Canadians in, but not as a corps. General Horne, a good friend of Sir Arthur's, called on the Corps Commander to advise him that two Canadian divisions were to be attached to the Fifth Army to take part in the Passchendaele battle. Replying, Sir Arthur advised General Horne that the Canadians would fight as a corps or not at all, and under no circumstances would they fight with the Fifth Army under Sir Hubert Gough.

That same evening, Currie was summoned to First Army Headquarters to see General Horne again. He returned shortly to tell his senior staff officer, Brigadier General de B. Radcliffe, that the Corps would be employed at Passchendaele under the Second Army, commanded by General Plumer.

This substitution of an army corps under a chosen commander, as required by General Currie, in place of two divisions assigned to General Gough, as ordered by the Commander-in-Chief, was surely unprecedented. But Currie was not through: he imposed further conditions.

The low-lying salient had been shelled, mined, and dug up almost continuously for four years, and the drainage system of what was reclaimed land had been completely destroyed. The area was a quagmire, pockmarked with deep shell-holes full of water and tangled lengths of barbed wire, where the risks of drowning were equal to the risks of enemy fire. German machine-gun posts were located in concrete pill-boxes, placed checkerwise on commanding positions, and were practically intact. What used to be roads leading up to the front lines were destroyed.

Far from relishing the new assignment, Currie thought the campaign of no value and less purpose. He had to obey orders, but was unwilling to expose his troops to needless slaughter, so insisted that before launching his attack there must be a complete survey of the area. The survey revealed the appalling conditions. Repairs must be made before he would concur in any action.

Impatient to get the attack under way, Sir Douglas called for a conference with the Canadian Corps Commander. Currie ordered all his heads of staff to attend, as well as commanders of the artillery, engineers, machine-guns, and medicals. All were familiar with the situation. General Brutinel was present at this conference. He relates that Sir Douglas, foiled by General Currie's determination, became very angry and expressed his displeasure forcibly, to which Sir Arthur replied in effect: "Sir, we are not trying to evade responsibilities. We have examined the situation and there is work to be done. What we undertake, we will do. Weather permitting, we'll take Passchendaele on the date *we* have suggested. I beg you, sir, to consider that my opinion is well founded, and as such should receive your approval."

Haig could only accept. Aided by Royal Engineers of the Second Army, Canadian sappers, pioneers, artillery, machine-gunners and infantry worked furiously to build and mend roads, set up battery positions, repair disabled guns. All this was accomplished under heavy shelling and bombs of mustard and "sneezing" gas. This latter penetrated gas-masks and caused the men to sneeze and vomit. Then the necessary removal of masks exposed them to the mustard. These preparations saved the lives of many in the forthcoming attacks, but accounted for over 1,500 casualties among the work parties.

Passchendaele Ridge was actually little more than a wrinkle in the flatness of the Salient but it commanded the important railway centre at Roulers. Although the original objective had long since been abandoned, capture of the Ridge offered some advantage since the Germans had been ordered to hold the position at all costs, and failure would damage their morale. According to prisoners, the word that the Canadians were taking over prompted the enemy to strengthen their defences and move up reinforcements.

Meanwhile, Canadian preparations for the opening attack went on feverishly, supplies and ammunition pouring up over the newly laid plank roads. In general, the plans for machine gun employment were similar to those used at Vimy, with harassing indirect fire, protective barrages and mobile guns. Added were sniping sections of four guns each, one or two to each divisional front. Human pack-mules manhandled the heavy guns through bog and shell-holes, waist- and even shoulder-high in water. Dogged determination and grim humour overcame difficulties.

Artillery plans, excellent as they had already proved, nevertheless underwent continual development. Currie was determined to provide massive support for his infantry and to destroy the fire-power of the enemy. Only a direct hit from a heavy shell could smash the five-foot walls of the German's concrete pill-boxes from which their machine-guns took such toll of the infantry.

Haig kept pressing Currie for an early attack, and although he would have liked a few more days, a compromise was reached by agreeing to launch the attack on October 26.

The offensive was planned in four stages. The first, October 26, 27 and 28, met with limited success: approximately 2,500 casualties and eight Canadians taken prisoner. In the second stage on the 30th the Canadians made gains and consolidated them; the day's casualties were 2,300 men and another eight men taken prisoner. On November 5 the 1st and 2nd Divisions relieved the 3rd and 4th and early in the morning of November 6 the infantry attacked again close behind their own powerful barrage.

In less than three hours the village of Passchendaele was in Canadian hands, but more than 2,200 men lay dead or wounded. Four days later, the final assault was made on the Ridge itself. A long day of bitter fighting in heavy rain brought to an end the Third Battle of Ypres. The village and Hill 52, the highest point on the northern end of the Ridge, were in possession of the Canadians—the captured area an exposed small thumb of a salient of its own, difficult to defend.

The Canadians once more had kept their promise. In two weeks of aggressive attacks they took Passchendaele Ridge. All services, co-ordinated and co-operating, made the Corps a tough hard-hitting fighting machine, but the cost was high—nearly 16,000 men were killed or wounded in the twenty-eight days the Corps occupied that front.

13

1917-18: CAMBRAI AND RE-ORGANIZATION

The name Passchendaele still blisters the tongue of many Britons. Lloyd George was to call it "grim, futile and bloody"; Winston Churchill, "a forlorn expenditure of valour and life without equal in futility." Critics say the campaign was ill-conceived and too late in getting started, and when failure of the initial objective was obvious, action should have been broken off. Instead, the Commander-in-Chief had stubbornly insisted on continuation, in spite of appalling weather and ground conditions, staggering losses, few gains and relatively insignificant objectives. This "wearing down the enemy" that Haig pursued so energetically was a costly business in the costliest currency a nation can spend.

The campaign was similar to that of the Somme the year before, and it was the repetition of such a slugging match that the public found hard to reconcile or forgive. Historians reveal a controversial spread in total figures, but British casualties for the three and a half months of Passchendaele were around a quarter of a million.

Sir Douglas Haig only gradually perceived that conditions had made a coastal breakthrough hopeless. He seems to have had a sincere belief that the prolonged offensive was justified because, unsolicited, he was relieving pressure on the French and seriously depleting the German army. But Passchendaele cracked his image in the eyes of the British, if not the world.

For Canadians, the Somme had been more of an ordeal. Relatively, losses at Passchendaele were higher—approximately 16,000 for the month as against nearly 25,000 in the Somme. But participation there had covered nearly three months of frustrating and repetitive attacks within an area of a few thousand yards, the brunt borne by the 4th Division in seven continuous weeks. On the other hand, at Passchendaele a year later, there was a marked change. There they fought as a corps: superior fire-power in both artillery and machine-guns supported the infantry in attack and defence. Currie had demanded, and been reluctantly accorded, time to improve back areas: thus it was possible to bring up guns and supplies and evacuate the wounded promptly. In the Somme it had been a major undertaking by six men to carry one stretcher back through the sea of mud, and many died in consequence. Results would have been very different without Currie's preliminary preparations. Resentful at the time, Haig forgave him when the Canadians delivered the Ridge as promised.

Another action took place that month that was of significance to later planning. The only Canadians taking part were the Cavalry. It was the attack on Cambrai by General Byng's Third Army which the Canadian Corps had anticipated before being sent to Passchendaele.

This action was to be a tank battle, an experiment eagerly sought by the Heavy Branch, now known officially as the Tank Corps. The ground around Cambrai was firm and unscarred, and the tanks were to be used in quantity—376 fighting vehicles smashing through to menace the western flank of the Hindenburg Line. Five infantry divisions would attack on the left, seize crossings over the St. Quentin Canal and strong-points in front of the city. Five divisions of cavalry, at last acting in their normal role, were to sweep through the breach made by the tanks and seize Cambrai.

The Canadian Cavalry Brigade was exuberant at being included in the plans. Trench warfare had permitted limited opportunities for cavalry action, and this was a glorious chance.

The battle began November 20. No preliminary bombardment alerted the enemy. For weeks the Tank Corps had secretly assembled the mass of 474 vehicles, 98 of them supply tanks, their rumbling approach drowned by the roar of British aircraft.

Brigadier General Elles, Commander of the Tank Corps, led the tanks in a terrifying sweep, advanced three miles on a six-mile front and breached the German line. In twenty-four hours they captured an area almost indentical in size with that captured in the whole Passchendaele offensive.

Unsupported on the left by artillery or tanks, the infantry had only partial success. Opportunity for the cavalry came on the second day. The 5th Cavalry Division moved forward, led by the Canadian Brigade. Then communications broke down, Cavalry H.Q. was so far to the rear that transmission of conditions took too long, and masses of horsemen waited for orders alongside the St. Quentin Canal.

The exception was the Fort Garry Horse. A bridge crossing the canal had collapsed under a tank, but "B" Squadron crossed over on a lock gate and went off on a battle of their own, out of communication and therefore beyond recall. When their squadron leader was killed, Lieutenant Harcus Strachan took command. They charged and overran a German battery, killing the gunners with their sabres, cut down parties of German infantry and spread panic throughout a considerable area. At dusk, perplexed by their isolation, they sheltered in a sunken road to rest. Then, as German patrols closed in, the horsemen stampeded their mounts to divert the enemy, drew their sabres and started back for the canal on foot.

Only about forty made it, but with them they brought sixteen prisoners captured in sharp fights on the way. Colonel H. I. Stevenson of Winnipeg, commanding the Garry's, was subsequently asked if Canadians did not know that the Cavalry Manual expressly states that horses cannot cross by a lock gate.

Colonel Stevenson replied: "Oh yes, we know, but our horses don't. They can't read."

Harcus Strachan was awarded the Victoria Cross.

But the battle for Cambrai deteriorated. There was no more mounted action for the Canadian Cavalry. The Royal Canadian Dragoons and Lord Strathcona's Horse were used dismounted and assigned defensive positions. The impetus was lost, and there were no reserves to consolidate gains. The enemy re-took them in powerful counter-attacks. Nevertheless the tanks had proved themselves and thereafter British G.H.Q. was more inclined to heed recommendations for tank employment.

According to General J. F. C. Fuller, Cambrai had been primarily conceived as a raid. The Tank Corps was concerned to learn that instead, it was to be a decisive battle. Reserves were lacking and Fuller himself doubted the ability of the mounted troops to accomplish anything decisive. His recommendation to keep reserves and not throw everything in at once was rejected. The operation, after all, was experimental, and the Tank Corps themselves, as well as the Third Army commanders, were novices in tank warfare. The cavalry commanders were completely out of their depth.

There is an interesting sidelight on this battle and its commander, revealed by a Canadian gunner, Colonel W. E. Harris of London, Ontario, who, as officer in charge of gas warfare, served on the headquarters staff under both Byng and Currie. He tells that soon after the battle General Byng visited Canadian Corps H.Q., and at his request a number of his former staff officers and commanders were invited to an informal meeting. There Sir Julian explained that he wanted his old comrades to know the reason for the failure of the Third Army at Cambrai—after all he had learned with the Corps, he was mortified to have seemed so incompetent and careless.

His own plan and orders had been scrapped, he said. Higher authority had imposed other plans, other orders. Artillery support for infantry was withdrawn; promised reserves had never appeared. Byng was not so much excusing himself as blowing off steam to friends he could trust to understand—whose good opinion he valued. The action at Cambrai could not help but damage it.

The Canadian Corps was now back on its old front besieging Lens. Here commanders assessed the recent battle at Passchendaele to find what could be learned from it.

By the winter of 1917-18 the manpower shortage was acute, the result of the killing-fests of the past three years. The Allied forces had a greater overall strength in men, and heavy and field artillery; the Germans greater superiority in infantry weapons such as trench mortars and machine-guns, heavy, medium and light.

Intelligence reports indicated that the Germans intended a vast offensive operation in the spring, bringing troops from Italy and the East. It was to be a desperate effort for a decisive victory before the Americans could take part.

British General Headquarters sought to solve the manpower problem at a conference of British commanders—army, corps, divisional and infantry brigadiers. At Le Touquet-Paris Plage, Brigadier General Bonham Carter of British G.H.Q. explained that the failing manpower situation required the reduction of brigade machine-gunners, in order to maintain a given number of rifles in depleted battalions.

Carefully and at length he placed this proposal before a frozen-faced audience. Misgivings were apparent, and expressed emphatically. Lieutenant-General Sir Hunter Weston (8th Army Corps) asked if the Canadian Machine Gun officer was present. He wasn't. The commanders then stated that nothing should be decided till they had heard Colonel Brutinel's views.

A wire summoned Brutinel to Le Touquet. He arrived next morning to be met by a staff officer, who took him at once to General Bonham Carter. This is Brutinel's own account:

General Bonham Carter said: "We've sent for you at the request of some of the corps commanders who'd like to hear your opinion. As you know, British Headquarters has looked at every angle of the problem and has arrived at certain conclusions. We expect you to support those conclusions."

I said: "Don't be too sure. I don't know what your conclusions are, but I certainly won't say anything of which I don't agree or approve. If you don't think I should go to the conference, tell me and my car will turn about, and I'll go back to my own headquarters."

Bonham Carter said: "No, no, you must come. The conference will start as soon as they know you're here."

I went into the conference room—a sort of theatre with a small stage—and Bonham Carter went on the stage and expressed again the views of G.H.Q. *and their proposals. Then General Hunter Weston said: "Now let's hear what Brutinel has to say to that!"*

I said: "Of course this proposal is tantamount to losing fire-power of a great many men so as to add men to do the fatigue work. What would you think of a manufacturer who, being short of hands to clean windows, decided to stop his great machines so as to relieve men for that purpose?"

Everyone laughed. I went on to say that the policy of reducing machine-guns would not remedy the shortage of men in infantry brigades, but would undoubtedly lower their fire-power. Instead, the number of machine-guns should be increased proportionately to maintain, if not improve their fire-power. The audience gave signs that they approved of the point of view, and one infantry brigadier stood up and said: "I'm an infantry commander and I've been dead against losing men to the machine-gunners, but I believe Brutinel's right. I say take whatever men you like from my brigade, as long as you give me more machine-gun support."

The conference ended as expected—inconclusively.

In January a Committee on Manpower explored the matter and the re-organization that followed reduced from twelve to nine the number of battalions in a British division, increasing the proportion of artillery and machine-guns to infantry. The inevitable delay in putting this into effect was one of the unfortunate factors in the German offensive in March.

With this reduction in British divisional strength, pressures were brought on Currie to follow suit, as the Australians had done earlier. Currie opposed them fiercely.

The first came from the War Office where Sir William Robertson was Chief of Imperial General Staff; the second from powerful Canadian political and military factions.

The Canadian Corps had four strong divisions in France. A fifth division in England, commanded by Major-General Garnet Hughes, was depleted by reinforcing the Corps, but still a division. By reducing the size of existing divisions, a sixth could be created from the leftovers, but six divisions were too many for one corps. This meant that a second corps must be formed. Two corps add up to one small army, with an approximate increase of 33 per cent in staff to administer both corps and an army headquarters—to say nothing of further ancillary services to complete a top-heavy formation.

With barely enough bodies to staff army headquarters, two corps headquarters, and corps troops, and to man six fighting divisions, there would be few left for reinforcements.

It is difficult to see Sir William's point. The change in the British forces entailed no such increases of headquarters or services, yet he was persistent in trying to bring General Currie into line. First he called on the Minister of State for the Colonies to approach the Governor General of Canada, which the Minister was discreet enough to refuse. Then he called on the High Commissioner for Canada, now Sir George Perley, who promised nothing.

Robertson's views were not shared by Haig or the British Prime Minister, so why did he persist? In any case, his efforts were unsuccessful, and in February Sir Henry Wilson replaced him as Chief of Imperial General Staff.

There was, however, much to be gained by the other wing of opposition. The creation of a Canadian army with two corps would open up a quantity of senior appointments and promotions—an army commander, two corps commanders, more divisional and brigade commanders, and ranking staff jobs galore, with a doubtful number of qualified officers to hold them. Sugar-plums like these enlisted support from many who should have known better. The heady thoughts of power, prestige, and pay befuddled reason.

Had the scheme been effected, probably Currie would have become Army Commander, since the combined weight of Haig and other British generals in the field was sufficient to outweigh his detractors. But Currie fought fiercely against it, submitting a plan of his own which could not have been more radically opposite.

Instead of splitting the Corps, Currie recommended that it be supplemented by using the 5th Division to add one hundred additional men to the forty-eight fighting battalions and to increase establishments of Corps troops. By this means the Corps gained fighting strength without adding any staff. This relatively reduced the administrative tail—a move as unpopular then as it would be today. It was certainly bitterly opposed by many influential people. These appealed to Lloyd George who refused to interfere.

Early in February Sir Arthur won his points after conferring with the Canadian Overseas Minister, now Sir Edward Kemp, and the G.O.C. Canadian Forces in the British Isles, Lieutenant-General Sir Richard Turner. The second army corps was not created and the increase in establishments was promised. But the cost in enemies was high; more and more of the uninformed were lining up against General Currie.

The 5th Division was disbanded after eleven of its battalions supplied drafts to units in France. The Canadian Corps emerged stronger than ever, its esprit de corps, morale and efficiency building up to a peak for great achievements in the last months of the war. With the extra men Currie effected his own re-organization within the Corps, supplementing the overall strength with some 14,000 men.

Passchendaele had shown the terrible strain on the infantry in supplying working parties for such services as engineers, signallers, and machine-gunners. These three arms, in addition to the infantry itself, were substantially increased to provide their own work parties.

To Brutinel was left the perfection of his own organization. The strength of each machine-gun battalion was increased from three to four companies, and an officer of the Machine Gun Corps visited the infantry battalions and hand-picked fifty men from each battalion. The number of machine-gun signallers was almost tripled.

General Currie submitted the new proposals to London with a covering letter stating that, in view of the urgency of the situation, he had already taken the necessary steps to implement them. By the time approval arrived from the Militia Department, the German storm had broken, and it was in the line, on the move, and at temporary halts that the re-organization of the machine-gun companies into battalions took place. Brutinel gives credit for this remarkable feat to "that born teacher," Captain Mark Marshall, now of Edmonton, and to his brigade major, Major G. Forster, who survived the war but died some years later.

The break-up of the 5th Division brought more anger and resentment against Currie, this time from men forced to leave regiments raised in provincial areas to which they felt they owed allegiance. But the Corps Commander believed that breaking up a battalion already in the field by replacing it with one coming from a particular region in Canada (which was the suggested alternative) would have been disastrous. Experience and battle honours had been building up for months and even years.

Currie won again, at further cost in enemies, but as he himself expressed it in a letter to the Overseas Minister: "I have found out, and so has everyone here, that men (no matter where they come from in Canada) soon become intensely proud of their battalions."

So it came to pass that men from all over Canada served together in units, fighting shoulder to shoulder, and getting to know and respect each other as individuals, as could have happened in no other way. French Canadians served with men from the Prairies, Maritimers with men from Ontario and British Columbia, all mixed up with a common bond in the unit, to fight with equal courage and skill.

14

1918: THE GERMAN OFFENSIVE AND THE BRITISH RETREAT

Although Haig did not interfere in feuds within the Canadian family, he did add to Currie's burden with a mild but relentless pressure to employ parts of the Corps outside the Corps area. The Canadians would not have done well dispersed, for they were a militia army, relatively free of military dogma, and had developed their own distinctive methods of warfare. To break up the Corps would mean the loss of that solidarity which had been the great factor in their success. General Plumer and General Byng recognized this, but not Sir Douglas, and in anticipation of the coming German offensive he tried again to break down Currie's stand.

Throughout the winter of 1917-18 the Canadians held the ground in the Vimy Ridge-Lens area. Behind them lay the only collieries still accessible to the Allies in Northern France, as well as the key centres of communication. It was one of the most vitally important areas in the whole line, and the Canadians spent their time organizing their defences. By spring they had built 250 miles of trenches, 300 miles of barbed-wire entanglements, 200 tunnelled machine-gun emplacements. Artillery was carefully sited and new battery positions built. There were also shelters, dugouts, and great supplies of ammunition, food, and water. The sector was so important to the French that their war cabinet sent a general to inspect the defences, who declared himself more than satisfied with the situation. For diversion, the troops turned to raids, and along with the 1st Motors, continually harassed the enemy.

Early in March, the Motors' commanding officer, ill and suffering battle fatigue, was replaced by Lieutenant-Colonel E. K. Walker, D.S.O., M.C., former commander of the machine-gun squadron, Canadian Cavalry Brigade. Brutinel, now a brigadier general, made the change of command so quickly and with so little warning that not even the C.O.'s batman knew he had left; thus the batman became the first casualty under Colonel Walker.

Walker was a huge man, six feet and more, weighing well over two hundred pounds. His predecessor, nerves taut, was a poor sleeper, and the batman was in the habit of creeping into the hut on his hands and knees each morning to collect tunic and boots for cleaning. On his first morning of command, Colonel Walker woke to see a shadowy figure crawling around his belongings and, suspecting he was there for no good purpose, pounced. What remained of the batman was evacuated for medical attention.

Walker was an excellent soldier, genial but a strict disciplinarian. Inevitably nicknamed Tiny, he used his command to advantage in tightening up training in the few days' grace before the Motors were thrown into action, suddenly and without notice.

The Canadian Corps was attached to the First Army (Horne) which was in position between the Second Army (Plumer) to the north and the Third Army (Byng) to the south. Beyond the Third was the Fifth Army (Gough). The Second Army held the strongest British sector in order to protect the Channel coast. Southward, the defences became increasingly weaker, for Haig believed that German gains here would be least harmful. The Fifth Army at the extreme southern end had been seriously depleted by increased commitments to the French.

By the second week in March Intelligence reported the Germans to be massing opposite the Third and Fifth Armies. On March 21, they struck under cover of a dense fog.

Shells rained down along the fronts of the two armies, with some threat made against the First. After bombardment came the assault. The rigid British defence, almost devoid of reserves, crumbled before the flexible infiltration tactics of the enemy who prodded the soft spots and broke through.

"We chop a hole," said Ludendorff. "The rest follows."

The Germans avoided the known strength of the Second Army and the area held by the Canadian Corps. Instead they concentrated on the Fifth and Third Armies which took the brunt of the attack. Enemy gains were appalling, with a twenty-five-mile penetration through the Fifth. After giving ground in the first shock of assault, the Third, with the First on its left, fought the Germans to a standstill, although outnumbered two to one.

On the morning of that momentous day, March 21, Sir Arthur Currie, summoned by Canadian Headquarters, had gone to London. He arrived in the afternoon and left again that same evening for France. He arrived back at Corps H.Q. on the night of the 22nd to find his command disintegrating.

When he had left, three of his divisions were in the line, the 2nd in reserve, but British G.H.Q., urgently calling for help, ordered the 1st and 2nd Divisions away as reserves, leaving the 3rd and 4th to hold 17,000 yards of front. In addition, the 1st Motor Machine Gun Brigade was rushed south to stem the tidal wave engulfing the Fifth Army. Three days later Currie was ordered to bring the 4th Division to join the 1st in reserve, with the command of the 3rd, still in the line, to pass to the Third Army. Canadian Corps Headquarters was to go into reserve.

For a short time Currie was virtually without a command, while his divisions rushed here and there over the countryside, often to arrive and be ordered to another position.

Sir Arthur vehemently protested this peremptory dispersal of his command, explaining that "one division thrown here and another there" could not do their best. The 1st and 2nd remained as reserves with the Third Army, but the 3rd and 4th Divisions were returned to Currie's command. With them he prepared to hold ten miles of vital front line.

In view of the tense and crucial situation, on March 28 Sir Arthur issued a Special Order to the Corps.

In an endeavour to reach an immediate decision, the enemy has gathered all his forces and struck a mighty blow at the British Army. Overwhelmed by sheer weight of numbers, the British Divisions in the line between the Scarpe and the Oise have fallen back fighting hard, steady and undismayed.

Measures have been taken successfully to meet this German onslaught. The French have gathered a powerful Army, commanded by a most able and trusted leader, and this Army is now moving swiftly to our help. Fresh British divisions are being thrown in. The Canadians are soon to be engaged. Our Motor Machine Gun Brigade has already played a most gallant part and once again covered itself with glory.

Looking back with pride on the unbroken record of your glorious achievements, asking you to realize that today the fate of the British Empire hangs in the balance, I place my trust in the Canadian Corps, knowing that where Canadians are engaged there can be no giving way.

Under the orders of your devoted officers in the coming battle you will advance or fall where you stand facing the enemy.

To those who will fall I say: "You will not die but step into immortality. Your mothers will not lament your fate but will be proud to have borne such sons. Your names will be revered forever and ever by your grateful country, and God will take you unto Himself.

Canadians, in this fateful hour, I command you and I trust you to fight as you have ever fought with all your strength, with all your determination, with all your tranquil courage. On many a hard-fought field of battle you have overcome this enemy. With God's help you shall achieve victory once more.

In that era, to men dedicated to the single purpose of defeating a common enemy, such words comforted and hardened their resolution. But was Currie, himself, as confident as he sounded?

Tempers were understandably short, for these were desperately anxious days, and Currie's opinion that "many British troops were not fighting well" was not confined to his diary, which also records: "Army Commander [Horne] called in the afternoon and resented any reflections on the fighting ability of the British formations." It must have been a turbulent interview.

The British were *not* fighting well, but it was due to lack of leadership and direction, not will. The Germans poured through Ludendorff's "hole," leaving most of the front line intact but making for the headquarters, the heart and brains of the army. The threat started a hurried withdrawal, first by brigade headquarters, then divisional, then corps. The forward troops were left without orders, support or communication. With the nerve centres gone, they were no longer an army, merely isolated bewildered individuals, who rallied together and bravely fought an enemy that appeared from all sides.

This was the melée to which General Currie refused to commit individual divisions, subject to the command of a general he considered incompetent.

Meanwhile the 1st Canadian Motor Machine Gun Brigade was in the middle of it all. The desperate appeal for the Motors was made on March 22, the day after the offensive was launched. General Brutinel tells the story:

On March 22, Brigadier General Dill, in charge of operations at British H.Q. *called on the telephone. He wanted to know if the Motors could be made ready for an early start next morning. He explained that he expected the employment of the brigade in the area where the Germans had broken through, and that instructions would be awaiting them at the City Hall in Amiens. I was to report personally to British* H.Q. *as soon as possible after the departure of the Brigade. A formal note would be sent General Sir Arthur Currie.*

Brutinel wasted no time. Advising General Webber, Canadian General Staff, of the situation, two batteries were ordered to withdraw from the line near Vimy. A full complement of munitions and supplies was issued and the brigade of five batteries under Colonel Walker was on its way by daybreak of the 23rd.

They reached Amiens shortly after noon, and minutes later were on their way to Villers-Bretonneux, arriving at General Gough's Army Headquarters by four p.m. There General Gough told Colonel Walker that the Motors were his last available reinforcements in a situation that was extremely serious. On their way again, they were in the front line and fighting by dusk, having travelled a hundred miles since dawn.

Before leaving for British G.H.Q., Brutinel issued orders for a constant flow of trained machine-gunners from the bases in France and England, to reinforce and maintain the fighting strength of the Brigade. After three and a half long years, the 1st Canadian Motor Machine Gun Brigade assumed the role for which it had been originally conceived.

No other formation in the Allied Forces could have done what the Motors did in those few crucial days of March and April, 1918, when the Germans nearly won the war on the Western Front. Mobility and fire-power were the secrets, but the miracle was that after more than three years of more or less static action, the Brigade was ready and able to swing into its destined role so perfectly. But the action was the reverse of that anticipated. Instead of breaking through enemy lines, they had to breast the tide of enemy advance, fighting delaying actions to cover a demoralized retreat.

Brutinel, reporting to General Dill at British H.Q., saw for himself the confusion, apprehension and general ignorance of conditions. Owing to the speed of the advance and the lack of communications, it was impossible to plot the situation on a map, and the exhausted staff officers were too weary to cope with the emergency adequately.

The Germans, using new and unorthodox tactics, evaded the hard core of the British front line and hit the weak spots.

Although the defending infantry were left almost intact, they had neither support nor orders, so disintegrated into pockets of desperate hand-to-hand fighting with little chance of survival. No communication, no support, no orders; it was every man for himself.

Brutinel had to ensure that supplies and equipment would be sent his brigade. These were in ample supply but could not be issued because all were earmarked for American divisions. Since there were no Americans at hand, he suggested they be diverted to where they would do the most good.

With the help of General Currie this was accomplished. Then as always the old problem of manpower cropped up. All services consulted reported their establishments were taxed to the utmost. No men were available for replacement.

Brutinel refused to accept defeat. What about the Horse Guards, mounting guard at Buckingham Palace? They could be quickly trained and made available for service at the front. This was not feasible. General Dill did not think that anyone at G.H.Q. would feel free to make such a suggestion to the King. Brutinel insisted.

"Obviously," he comments, "Nobody there had properly appraised the character of the King."

General Brutinel believed that if a special appeal was made, it would not be dismissed lightly, and he pressed his point. Within a few hours the War Office had passed on the request. Without delay the reply was received and the order issued.

"The Horse Guards will be ready to leave tomorrow."

Brutinel met them at Boulogne and arranged with the Machine Gun School to give them a short intensive course in preparation for their new role. The 1st Motors' orders were specific: to get in touch with the enemy, kill as many as possible and delay his advance.

The Canadian official history states:

The assistance given by the Motor Machine Gun Brigade to General Gough's exhausted and disorganized divisions had been far out of proportion to the size of such a comparatively small unit. Its officers and men had been trained to fight on their own initiative—training which bore good results when orders could not reach them, and headquarters of divisions and infantry brigades, continually on the move, could not be found.

That was how they fought; not as a brigade, but independently as single cars, sometimes two cars, or perhaps a couple of batteries. Frequently they fought dismounted. As they carried their own supplies it was comparatively easy to dig in and get all their ammunition and equipment into position.

The Brigade consisted of eight armoured cars and twelve specially constructed light trucks. Each vehicle had two guns, ammunition, extra petrol, and enough food for the fourteen N.C.O.'s and men. Two cars made a section under a lieutenant, two sections a battery, commanded by a captain. In all, the five batteries had twenty cars, forty guns and a complement of 280 men; also a section of motor cyclists of some fifty-one scouts who doubled as dispatch riders and signallers. These were the "eyes" of the Brigade—keeping the machine-gunners constantly and accurately informed.

Broadly, the unit was ordered to fill gaps occurring at any needful point on the army front. Tactics to be employed were: get in touch and co-operate with the nearest infantry; establish machine-gun positions in depth; support machine-gun posts by armoured car action. Accordingly, they made forays down side roads, spraying enemy garrisons with a hail of bullets as they passed through. At one crossroads, they took on a whole German regiment which finally broke and ran. Shifting here and there to trouble spots, or holding a position for hours while the British retired, they beat the Germans back, inflicting terrible losses but suffering them too.

In the afternoon of March 24, a battery under Captain E. H. Holland and another under Captain W. Nicholson were on their way to prevent an enemy crossing at Clery and Ham, and had to buck a motley stream of vehicles leaving the front. They pulled off to high ground and prepared to cover the retreat of the infantry. The two batteries fought fiercely, inflicting heavy punishment on the advancing enemy and using hand grenades as the Germans closed in, nearly surrounding them.

By this time several guns were knocked out and numbers of men casualties, including Captain Holland who was fatally wounded. Captain Nicholson ordered three cars to fall back because of the intense shelling—a fourth was too close to a dump of blazing explosives. Two men tried to move it and were killed. Two others got it away. With four guns out of action Captain Nicholson ordered his battery to retire to a trench fifty yards in the rear from where they covered the withdrawal of the trench's occupants, the 15th Cheshire Regiment.

By five o'clock only two guns remained in action. The infantry had pulled out, but the machine-gunners held on till practically overrun. Out of a battery of fifty men only eight were left, and these crawled from the trench and ran down the road. In the last few moments Captain Nicholson was severely wounded, but they all reached the remaining car. This ended the first day's fighting of two batteries, and Captain Nicholson's participation in the war, for he lost an arm.

An armoured car's maximum speed was 25 miles an hour, fast for those days, and on occasion they created havoc in enemy ranks, particularly in villages where the troops could not disperse. Early in the morning of March 25 two or three hundred Germans, exhausted after crossing the Somme River, were strung out along both sides of the main road through the village of Cizancourt. Two cars and six scouts on motor-bikes suddenly appeared, catching the enemy completely by surprise. Machine-guns killed a large number, the others bolted in every direction. Cars and scouts left the village without losses.

s.o.s. calls for the Motors were numerous and frequent, and the enemy used every means it could to destroy the marauding brigade, sweeping the roads with shell-fire and sending planes over to strafe them. Planes came off second best when the machine-gunners turned on them. During those terrible days, the Motors gave direction and confidence to a disorganized Fifth Army whose battle line had dissolved into unrelated groups rallying around an officer or a machine-gun and fighting for their lives.

General Brutinel maintained for the Brigade a constant flow of trained reinforcements. Many had no battle experience, but, fighting side by side with veterans they were quick to learn, and if lucky, soon became veterans themselves. Supplies were maintained too, and the Motors believed in helping themselves.

One captain solved the problem when he sought replacement of two guns and ammunition from a British Ordnance Depot. In the face of the enemy's advance, the major in charge and his staff were getting ready to clear out what stores they could. The M.G. officer asked for supplies—six guns and ammunition to offset future losses.

"Who are you?" asked the major. "Where's your authority?"

"Haven't any," replied the machine-gunner. "We're fighting a rear-guard action and the enemy is pressing."

"Can't issue guns or ammunition without proper authority from Corps Headquarters."

With a twist of his head, the captain summoned his crew close and pulled his revolver.

"This is my authority. Get on with it!" he snapped.

The ordnance personnel stared open-mouthed as their major sputtered at the bristling captain, surrounded by his grinning crew.

"You can't do that! I'll place you under arrest!"

"Not if you're dead, you won't! Get out of my way!"

The major fell back and the ordnance men meekly supplied the requirements before withdrawing to a safer area.

While the Motors fought many actions, one victory they could not claim.

Near Villers-Bretonneux two armoured cars, expecting an enemy advance, covered the road in a rearguard action. The Germans failed to appear, and after a long wait, the machine-gunners reconnoitred, first on the flanks, then forward. The advancing Germans had found a warehouse, its personnel departed, leaving shelves piled high with hundreds of cases of assorted spirits, stocked for sale to various officers' messes. Weary, yet jubilant with success, the Germans were celebrating too early and too much, killing bottle after bottle in carefree abandon. There was enough and more to spare, and as more troops arrived, they too joined in the fun.

The Motors withdrew without firing a shot—perhaps with a degree of wistful envy—but taking advantage of the lapse.

The tale of Harry Pepper's ostrich originated about this time at Villers-Bretonneux. Pepper was an old Yukoner, who overheard his battery commander say there was a live ostrich in a private menagerie nearby, and it would make a good mascot.

"What's an ostrich, sir?" asked Pepper.

"It's a kind of big bird," replied the officer.

Pepper resolved to get the big bird and surprise the battery, but the big bird surprised Pepper. In their brief encounter the ostrich kicked and Pepper won the distinction of becoming the first and only one of the Motors to be hospitalized by an ostrich.

For over two weeks the 1st C.B.M.G.B. fought day or night and often both, with little respite. Their combination of initiative, daring and stability steadied demoralized troops and gave leadership and cohesion to brave men, eager to fight. When they were ordered to rejoin the Canadian Corps in the second week in April, many familiar faces were missing. Casualties had claimed many of the originals, but using machines in lieu of manpower, they had inflicted terrible damage on the enemy, stemming their victorious advance over a 35-mile front.

Another Canadian formation participating in those ten crucial days of March was the Cavalry Brigade, which was not under the jurisdiction of the Canadian Corps. There had been few opportunities for cavalry to fight as such, but these Canadians had seen as much conflict as any, fighting dismounted wherever needed, frequently beside the Canadian infantry. Now they played a dual role. On March 22, eight hundred cavalrymen, dismounted, helped cover the retirement of the British 18th Division. A mounted detachment of two hundred joined three hundred British cavalrymen in re-establishing broken infantry lines and making small-scale counter-attacks against greatly superior forces. Lieutenant F. M. W. Harvey—already a V.C. winner—led a squadron of Strathcona's against a German-held village, capturing three times the strength of his squadron. It was so far forward that following French troops "captured" them, convinced they were Germans masquerading as Canadians.

Attached for a time to French cavalry in harassing raids against advancing Germans, the Brigade returned to British command on March 29 to fight a three-day battle for Bois de Moreuil and Rifle Wood. These German-held forests provided full observation of the roads out of Amiens and were vital if the city was to be held. The Fort Garry Horse, the Royal Canadian Dragoons and the Lord Strathcona's Horse, supported by two batteries of Royal Canadian Horse Artillery, fought full strength here, mounted and dismounted. The battle raged against powerful enemy resistance. Massed machine-gun fire menaced the Brigade until Lieutenant Gordon Flowerdew led his Strathcona section in a gallant charge, their sabres literally cutting machine-gunners to pieces. Flowerdew did not live to receive the Victoria Cross awarded him, but the Woods were taken on April 1 and Amiens was saved.

Not to be forgotten were the four hundred officers and men of the 2nd Battalion Canadian Railway Troops, who were called upon to man the Amiens defence line and suffered casualties in the heavy shelling.

By mid-April General Currie had three of his divisions back (the 2nd was to stay with the Third Army until July) and was holding nearly twenty miles of front—a fifth of the whole British line. The Battle of the Lys to the north of Vimy placed the Canadians in a perilously vulnerable salient, but the Germans made no aggressive attack there.

Canadian participation in the March offensive not only went unrecognized; a distorted impression prevailed that the Canadians had stood back and refused to help at a crucial time. Sir Douglas Haig gave weight to this belief with misleading entries in his diary. His anger is apparent. On April 18 he writes:

Currie is suffering from a swollen head, Horne thinks. He lodged a complaint when I ordered the Canadian divisions to be brought out of the line in order to support the front and take part in the battle elsewhere. He wishes to fight only as "a Canadian Corps" and get his Canadian representative in London to write and urge me to arrange it. As a result the Canadians are together holding a wide front near Arras but they have not yet been in the battle.

Later, on July 19, he writes of an interview with Major-General the Honourable S. C. Mewburn, Canadian Minister of Defence:

. . . I told the Canadian Minister that the British Army alone and unaided by Canadian troops withstood the first terrific blow made by 80 German divisions on March 21 until May 27, when the Aisne attack was launched. . . . During the severe fighting the Canadian Corps had not once been engaged—because the Canadian Government only wished it to be engaged as a Corps.

But *The Canadian Forces in the War* written by Professor F. H. Underhill and included in a volume of "The Empire at War" edited by Sir Charles Lucas, gives a more accurate account.

For nineteen days that unit [the Motors] *was continuously in action north and south of the Somme, fighting against overwhelming odds. Using to the utmost its great mobility it fought over two hundred square miles of territory. . . . The losses suffered amounted to about 75 per cent of the trench strength of the unit.*

The Commander-in-Chief was regrettably ill-informed.

15

TRAINING FOR OPEN WARFARE

By April 5 the Germans had failed to take Amiens. Although the breakthrough penetrated twenty-five miles at that point, it was stopped at Villers-Bretonneux and Moreuil Wood—a dozen miles or so in front of Amiens—and the enemy turned their attention elsewhere.

Haig desperately needed reinforcements. His armies were greatly outnumbered. The French, still under Pétain, were concerned with the safety of Paris and sent less than half the number of divisions he asked for. The Commander-in-Chief was by now openly declaring himself in favour of a unified command under General Foch as Commander-in-Chief of the Allied armies, and early in April this appointment was made. But Foch proved no more helpful in providing further reinforcements. The enemy attacked persistently, now to the north in the sector held by the First and Second Armies. Here they pushed the British back, capturing Armentières, Messines, the eastern face of Passchendaele Ridge and much of the forward slope towards Ypres—all territory that had been dearly bought in past engagements.

To Sir Arthur Currie, who had grieved over the useless battles won by Canadians at high cost, the loss of this ground was a particularly bitter pill, and he made no secret of it as General Pershing, the

United States commander who visited the Corps on April 20, records.

One attack started near the La Bassée Canal where the line was occupied by a Portuguese Division, a token force sent when Portugal joined the Allied side. They had purposely been assigned to a quiet part of the front, but again the Germans attacked the weak spot with a punishing bombardment.

A Canadian Cyclist Battalion went up to support the Portugese, leaving their bikes in the rear. They hardly reached the forward area before they met the defenders, streaming back in a most disorganized withdrawal—"running like hell" as the Canadians reported it.

The Cyclists rapidly took over and when later relieved by a British battalion, they were enraged to find their bikes gone. Trudging back through the small villages where they were billeted, they heard from the villagers how the Portuguese heroes had saved the day, and in gratitude had been lent the bicycles. From that time on, the Canadian Cyclists had little good to say of the "Pork and Cheese soldiers." This derogatory term became so prevalent that an order came out worded by some tongue-in-cheek staff officer, stating that "the practice of calling our gallant Portuguese allies Pork and Cheese will stop forthwith." This of course had the reverse effect: Pork and Cheese they remained.

The enforced withdrawals of the British on both sides of the Canadian-held position left the latter in a dangerously deepening salient. On April 19 Foch relented and sent French troops to bolster the northern sector of the British line. But in the following week Ludendorff struck on the south again, threatening Amiens. This time they captured Moreuil and Villers-Bretonneux, but in a counter-attack next day Villers-Bretonneux was recaptured and Amiens remained in Allied hands, as the Germans turned their attention north again, toward Ypres. This time, there were adequate French reinforcements and as the enemy troops were now close to exhaustion, Ludendorff called off the offensive. There had been terrible losses on both sides but the German gamble had only partially failed. The Channel ports were saved, but the line had been forced back in many places beyond that of 1914, when the first great sweep was made.

The enemy still held the initiative, and throughout the spring and early summer they exploited their successes, inflicting many casualties on both French and British forces, but the Canadians had no part in these battles. The Germans never attacked the thinly-held Canadian line, but by constant harassment and raids, the Canadians prevented the enemy from withdrawing troops to reinforce elsewhere. It was on Foch's explicit orders that they were relieved early in May and placed in reserve.

Meanwhile General Currie had been going ahead with his reorganization. In an address to his G.O.C.'s he is reported to have said bluntly:

I shall not wait until such organization is sanctioned by higher authorities, but proceed immediately if I can obtain machine-guns. Official sanction can come later. I want 2,400 men and I propose that each battalion give fifty of their best who will go on the strength of the Machine Gun Corps.

That Corps now had their companies grouped into four battalions of four companies each, drawing the additional men from the infantry. It was a considerable feat to absorb so many men and train them right in the line, but it was done, and in the doing the Machine Gunners retained the wonderful spirit of the old compact companies.

Brutinel prepared a memorandum which the Corps Commander issued setting forth the Corps policy with respect to machine-gun troops.

The Machine Gun Corps at last was recognized as a distinctive arm with tactics of its own. Now they were divisional troops, under the command and tactical control of a divisional machine-gun commander, similar to the artillery command. This policy was far in advance of British G.H.Q., who months later authorized the adoption of the Canadian principles of command and tactics.

Mobility being the crux of tactics, attention was given to expanding and re-organizing the mechanized arm of the Machine Gun Corps, and the 1st Motors were divided to form two motor machine-gun brigades—the 1st and 2nd—their ranks supplemented by the 17th, 18th, and 19th Machine Gun Companies, each comprising five eight-gun batteries. A Mechanical Transport Company, to administer and maintain transport, became part of the Corps.

To each of the two motor machine-gun brigades were added a detachment of cyclists with nine Lewis guns, and two sections of six-inch trench mortars mounted on trucks. This whole unit was named the Canadian Independent Force, but was more commonly called Brutinel's Brigade. Brutinel commanded it, and he was probably one of the busiest brigadier generals on the front, since he also commanded the Canadian Machine Gun Corps Headquarters. There, a small but able staff headed by one major (Forster) and one captain

(J. K. Lawson, later a brigadier, who was killed in 1941 at Hong Kong) handled routine administration, while Brutinel directed the Motors in the forefront of battle.

Machine-gun schools were greatly expanded to train reinforcements and it was at this time that friction reached boiling point at British General Headquarters' Machine Gun Schools. Selected Canadians were ordered to attend them in the hope of maintaining a unity of doctrine, but from the first the difference in doctrines was widespread. More than likely, the Canadians criticized, vocally and obnoxiously. Certainly they complained that the courses were a waste of time. The School staffs, equally vocal, resented criticism from "colonials, Canadians in particular." Friction finally developed to a degree that could not be ignored by the Higher Command.

Brutinel took the matter up with the Corps Commander, who took it up with the First Army Commander, who took it up with the Commander-in-Chief. Sir Douglas had already received reports from the other side. Could a curriculum be submitted, he asked, revising and implementing the machine-gun courses of the British General Headquarters' Schools? It could.

General Brutinel was ordered to submit a program of re-organization. The project was prepared and submitted within twenty-four hours, together with a list of British officers familiar with Canadian doctrines and able to re-organize and lecture competently. The Commander-in-Chief adopted these suggestions and Brigadier General Ironside was selected to supervise the whole operation. Thereafter the courses ran smoothly. Ironside had been General Staff Officer with the 4th Canadian Division, and knew something of these wild colonials and their machine-gun beliefs.

An army learns more quickly by defeat than by victory, and there were many changes that spring. The unity of command under General Foch was a great morale booster to the Canadians at least. They had fought so hard and so long, see-sawing back and forth over the same desolate land, where an advance of a few hundred yards was hailed as a great victory. It didn't take a military expert to see there was something wrong at the top. In fact, the military experts seemed to be the last to see it.

Perhaps the Canadians felt the frustration most keenly. They had faith in their own leaders, for since Vimy Ridge the Corps had never looked back, but they felt the stalemate could never be broken with multi-headed armies, even the influx of Americans. With the Chief of the Allied Armies, Generalissimo Foch, in the driving seat, the prospects brightened considerably.

Brutinel notes:

Characteristically, as soon as Foch was appointed, and regardless of the fact that everything appeared to be crumbling away before the German offensive, he gave orders for the Canadian Corps to be withdrawn from the line as soon as possible and to be placed in reserve in the St. Pol en Ternoise area. The French Tenth Army was concentrated in the same sector, and General Foch ordered that these two forces start immediate training for open warfare.

In May the Generalissimo sent for General Brutinel, meeting him at St. Pol.

He told me frankly that the information concerning the Canadian Forces, which he'd obtained from the British General Staff, was not sufficient for him to form a definite opinion regarding the value of the Canadians in offensive warfare.

I replied substantially: Since their arrival in France the Canadians have given abundant proof of their initiative and of their intelligent estimation of the problems arising out of many situations. They have initiated the raids on enemy lines—breaking the local stalemate. They have always carried out objectives assigned them—the taking of Vimy Ridge and Passchendaele demonstrate precisely what I mean. They have never lost ground or guns to the enemy without recovering their losses themselves within 48 hours, except in the Ypres Salient when it took them thirteen days to recover lost ground and two field guns, taken by the Germans on the 2nd of June, 1916—ample proof of their tenacity.

General Brutinel's opinion might be considered prejudiced, but he was too good a soldier to over-estimate the capabilities of his troops. General Foch listened attentively.

"I see you have an excellent opinion of your Corps," Brutinel reports him as saying. "I would like to have concrete knowledge of the compostion of the Canadian Corps. Can you give me this information?"

"Yes, sir, I can," replied Brutinel, "and I will do so as soon as I have been authorized by General Currie."

"Yes, yes. That is what I would expect you to say. Can you give me the information I want—say inside of three or four days? I'd like also to know the possibilities of maintaining substantially the fighting strength of the Corps for some time, in case of hard fighting."

General Brutinel reported the conversation to General Currie who at once ordered the preparation of statements dealing with all arms and services. He also instructed his Deputy Assistant Adjutant General, Major Wilfred Bovey, to report on the possibilities of reinforcements. These documents were in General Foch's hands four days later.

Foch delved deeply into the organization, record, and performance of the Canadian Corps and through the summer months watched it with an eagle eye. As a visitor at Corps H.Q. he got his information where he could find it, brushing aside military etiquette to get at the facts. Shortly before the operation of August 8, Brutinel reports the Generalissimo as saying in a private conversation that the Canadian Corps was "an Army second to none, deriving its immense strength from the solid organization of each of its component parts, welded together in battle conditions."

In the last hundred days of the war, the Corps' performance confirmed his opinion.

16

THE BATTLE OF AMIENS

So far the Americans had not taken a major role. By April they had nine combat divisions (larger than even the Canadian) in France and more arrived in the following months till October, when there was a total of forty-two. In actions that spring and summer they were engaged at the southern end of the battle line, covering the threat to Paris, and while they fought gallantly, as green troops against an experienced enemy, their casualties were heavy.

Meanwhile the new look under the supreme commander General Foch took effect at once. Out of the line from the second week in May, the Canadians concentrated on their re-organization and intensive training for open warfare. This indicated an offensive role at last. After the long defensive strain of the Vimy sector there was a dash and exhilaration as they practised with tanks, planes, new enlarged formations of the machine-gun battalions, and the two new motor machine-gun brigades. Brutinel issued specific orders to machine-gun officers to use their own initiative and a degree of latitude in the employment of their weapons. This was to pay dividends in the last hundred days of the war.

In Canada meantime, the Military Service Act (conscription) had been in effect for some months, and beginning that summer draftees joined and trained with the Corps. Commanders brooked no criticism or recrimination from the veterans, and the integrated draftees seemed to conform to the spirit of the Corps, fighting later with skill and courage. But with them came the ugly rumours current in Canada about Sir Arthur Currie.

Early in July an engagement took place that wiped out the rancour of the Australians for the Tank Corps, incurred in 1917 after the disastrous battle at Bullecourt. It was indirectly related to the Canadians who had observers present.

In June 1918 Tank Corps Commander Elles persuaded Australian Corps Commander Monash to let him demonstrate the value of tanks properly employed. After three weeks of combined training, the Australians, supported by tanks, attacked the town of Hamel, a German-held salient important because it was within effective field-gun range of the Amiens marshalling yards. The Australians had been attempting to take it for some weeks, with mounting casualties.

This was not a major engagement, but the psychological results were of great importance and far-reaching. The infantry was reduced to a minimum, the tanks used in quantity. Surprise was the main element with maximum machine-gun support; no wire-cutting—the tanks would see to that.

Zero hour was three a.m. on July 4. By five a.m. the battle was over, all objectives achieved. To consolidate the line, supply tanks arrived loaded with front-line Australian troops, barbed wire, bombs, ammunition, drinking water and unofficially, a number of bottles of whisky for celebration.

Casualties were remarkably light. Out of ten battalions of infantry there were 672 men killed and wounded. Of 60 tanks, 58 reached their objective and 55 returned, the other five being salvaged later. Not a single officer or man in the tanks was killed and only eight were injured seriously.

This battle had a profound effect on the Higher Command and on subsequent tank employment in the autumn offensives, although the Higher Command too often lessened effectiveness by thrusting an interfering finger into the pie of tactical planners.

Foch pursued his command with confidence and authority, introducing the long-ignored principles of war—surprise, secrecy, and deception. Hitherto, projected attacks had been common knowledge to friend and foe alike. Troops discussed them openly in estaminets and billets; it was inevitable that the enemy knew them too. Now a rigid security clamp was enforced, and pasted in all rank's pay-books were the words: KEEP YOUR MOUTH SHUT!

The Canadians' "rest period" of two months was actually a time of gruelling training. It came to an end on July 15 when the Corps was ordered to the Arras sector in anticipation of attacks on objectives called Orange Hill and Monchy-le-Preux.

But on the 20th, General Currie was told privately that an attack was to be made early in August in front of Amiens. It was intended to relieve pressure on Amiens and free the Amiens-Paris railway. The Canadian Corps was to be used, but with limited objectives.

The plan was a closely guarded secret. In order to mislead both friend and foe, preparations went on near Arras. For further deception, some troops were dispatched north to the Ypres sector, simulating an advance party, where they industriously appeared to be making preparations for battle. If not wholly deceived, the enemy was nevertheless confused.

Senior commanders were soon advised of the true intentions but elaborate precautions at deception went on, moving troops north by day, returning them by night. The troops, themselves bewildered, put it all down to "some bloody fool who couldn't make up his mind."

Originally the Higher Command intended to make this offensive the final battle of that year, then sit tight and wait for the Americans. It was General Currie who, dreading the prospect of another winter in the trenches for his men, pointed out that even on a quiet front, casualties averaged two hundred a day. If the Canadians were successful at Amiens, he said, then their success must be pressed, continuing the offensive in the hope of winning the war before Christmas.

The suggestion was well received and Foch's plan became an all-out attack by combined Allied forces. At zero hour, not before, a dense artillery barrage would begin, and the infantry advance under its cover.

Hoping that the Germans believed they were at Arras and going to Ypres, the Canadians moved into the Amiens area only a couple of days before August 8, sheltering in woods and camouflaging positions. The weather co-operated for once, being cloudy and foggy, preventing aerial observation. All fires were forbidden—only cold food available. To most of the men their actual location on the map was unknown till the last minute of briefing, and this encouraged and excited them. If they were ignorant of their position, surely the Germans were too.

On the night of August 7-8 the artillery came into position. None of their guns had been registered, but Colonel McNaughton, in an unprecedented feat, had the angles and ranges carefully plotted beforehand, thus ensuring the complete surprise and success of the opening barrage.

That same night the infantry moved into the line. General Lipsett's 3rd Division, with the longest distance to march, arrived just twenty minutes before zero hour. As each division completed assembly, it reported to Corps Headquarters with the code words "Llandovery Castle," the name of a Canadian hospital ship, sunk weeks previously, with only twenty-four survivors. In the hearts of many Canadian soldiers that August morning was the determination to avenge this outrage.

Covered as much as possible by the noise of aircraft, the tanks rumbled up just after four o'clock. At precisely 4:20 a.m., in a heavy mist, 900 guns opened their barrage and the infantry started forward.

The Canadians, under the British Fourth Army, were in the centre of the attacking line, with the Australians on their left and the French First Army on their right. To them fell the responsibility of striking the main blow, with a planned penetration of eight miles—their front broadening fan-shaped as they advanced.

The Canadian Independent Force was on the right flank, the connecting link with the French Army. This was ground they knew well, for it was here the Motors had held up the German army in the March Retreat five months before.

The attack was a complete surprise to the Germans. Caught off guard, they fought fiercely. The Canadians advanced so rapidly that the artillery had difficulty keeping in touch, and parties of gunners went forward to turn captured guns against the retreating enemy. Batteries moved forward at least five times during the day. Even the battalions in reserve found themselves involved in sharp encounters with German detachments, by-passed in the push.

The early mist was of great advantage to the infantry, but handicapped the artillery, and was most confusing for the tanks where vision was limited at best. Many lost direction.

One innovation that proved less than successful was the use of tanks to transport machine-gun crews ahead of the main body of infantry. Each of the twenty-one supporting tanks of the 4th Division lifted an infantry officer, a scout and three machine-gun detachments from the 4th Machine Gun Battalion.

The tanks were to head for the day's objective, eight miles forward, and unload the passengers. With half the tanks remaining in support, the rest were to return to assist the main body of infantry. But the eight-mile ride with deviations took better than two hours. The passengers, jolted in cramped quarters and unused to the heat and fumes, became sick, and some passed out. More than half had to get out and follow on foot where they were subjected, along with the tanks, to enemy fire. Ten tanks were knocked out, the inmates burned or shot down escaping. Eleven reached the objective, but enemy fire was so hot that seven withdrew. Only four got gun crews into action.

Elsewhere, however, the tanks did yeoman service and answered numerous calls to dislodge enemy strong-points. It was here that the whippet tanks were first used, at the breath-taking speed of seven miles an hour. Along the whole front, all arms functioning with wonderful co-ordination, the troops advanced with surprisingly few casualties and an exhilaration never before equalled.

Straddling the Amiens-Roye road the Independent Force and a detachment from the 3rd British Divisional Cavalry (for the time being under Currie's command) protected respectively the right and left flanks of the Canadians and General Debeney's French First Army. The village of Mézières offered stiff resistance to the French, but the Independent Force participated with overhead fire, a detachment of cyclists and a machine-gun unit, capturing the town and compelling the Germans to withdraw.

In another enemy-occupied village, one of Brutinel's motor cyclists, scouting ahead, rode through the main street, as surprised as the Germans at finding himself there. Steering with one hand he emptied his automatic into the gaping Jerries as he sped furiously down the road. Not far behind came an armoured car and more of his pals, to whom the demoralized enemy willingly surrendered.

The Australians, on the Canadian left flank, had to attack over particularly difficult ground, the Somme River valley with its numerous ravines and hideous memories of 1916. Their advance was more limited, hampered, too, by the reverses of the British on their left who had been fighting for several days. Nevertheless, while all objectives were not reached, success of the first day's battle was well beyond the greatest hopes. It sealed the fate of the German army:

the "Black Day" Ludendorff called it, when they suffered their greatest defeat so far, with crushing effect on morale.

On the 9th, the advance continued, but more slowly. The front had reached the old 1917 line of overgrown trenches and wire, which lent themselves to stubborn defence. Fighting was harder; the attack late and ragged in starting owing to a change of mind and orders at Fourth Army Headquarters.

According to General Currie after the war:

The success of the Australians and Canadians was so startling . . . that in my opinion G.H.Q. *had no definite ideas what to do. . . . Senior staff officers hurried up from* G.H.Q. *to see me and ask what I thought should be done. They indicated quite plainly that the success had gone far beyond expectations and that no one seemed to know just what to do. I replied in the Canadian vernacular; "the going seems good; let's go on."*

But indecision was evident: the push lacked the earlier precision and unity.

Fortunately the Germans made no serious attempt to counter-attack, but fresh reserves were being rushed to bolster the defence; resistence was stiffening. The advance that day on the Canadian front was only four miles; casualties were heavy, particularly for the Australian Corps. By the 10th, the impetus had slowed down considerably.

In this battle the cavalry took an active part with a courage and dash that deserved success, but this was no cavalryman's war. In a gallant but heartbreaking charge at Zed Wood, they were cut to pieces, floundering over old grass-grown trenches against concealed barbed wire, at the mercy of German machine-gunners.

But near Rosières they had more success. Ordered to cut the railway line into the town, they made a daring attack, cut the line, destroyed a big twelve-inch railway howitzer and took a large number of prisoners, including the staff of a new hospital train caught on the wrong side of the blown rail. The doctors and nurses were sent home through Holland, but first they were led past cages full of thousands of prisoners of war and huge stacks of captured guns. Their reports when they reached Germany would not help morale.

Elsewhere the cavalry rounded up prisoners and struck terror into isolated bands of Germans, but in battle, machines and guns took terrible toll of man and beast.

The end of the Battle of Amiens came on August 11 with a return to the old static misery of trench warfare. Further local engagements took place, but they were costly and achieved little.

While room for improvement had been noted, the Canadian commanders had reason to feel satisfaction at the way the battle had gone. Among the many congratulatory messages, perhaps the one that counted most was from their former commander. General Sir Julian Byng told General Currie that the Canadian performance at Amiens was the "finest operation of the war."

As the Corps moved to new fields to conquer, Sir Arthur told his men: "This magnificent victory has been won because your training was good, your discipline was good, your leadership was good. Given these three, success must always come."

They had defeated elements of fifteen German divisions (completely routing four) penetrated fourteen miles on a front up to 10,000 yards (an area of more than sixty-seven square miles), captured 9,000 prisoners, 200 guns of various calibre and over 1,000 machine-guns and trench mortars. The cost? Approximately 11,000 killed and wounded.

There was now some difference of opinion among the Higher Command about continuing the action, though all agreed that the success at Amiens warranted Currie's previous suggestion to push on and finish the war. The question was, where?

The Germans were now entrenched and reinforced. Aerial photographs showed the strength of their positions. The Allied forces were exhausted; the element of surprise was gone. General Foch was anxious to push on there and then, but Haig was against it. When General Debeney—French First Army—asked that the attack be postponed, and General Currie opposed continuation of the offensive, Foch concurred with the overall opinions to press on another front. Even during the so-called lull-in-fighting interim, between August 11 and 19, bitter local engagements had resulted in over two thousand casualties to the Canadians alone.

Leaving the 1st and 4th Divisions to follow later, the Canadian Corps returned to the Arras sector on August 19. Here their position was bounded on the north by the Scarpe River, and chequerboard in front were Orange Hill, Monchy-le-Preux and Chapel Hill. They were now confronted with the task of breaking through the Hindenburg Line to capture Cambrai. This was a formidable undertaking with three sets of almost impregnable enemy lines, Fresnes-Rouvroy, Drocourt-Quéant and the Canal du Nord. On August 22 General Currie called his commanders together and outlined the plan.

17

THROUGH THE HINDENBURG LINE TO CAMBRAI

It was no easy assignment in view of the elaborate system of defence the Germans had constructed in the winter of 1917. This was the line from which the enemy started their successful offensive the previous March. Now they were back to it, after their black week in August.

The heavily fortified connecting trench or "switch" between Drocourt and Quéant was the pivot or hinge on which the two great German armies moved—Crown Prince Rupprecht's on the right, Crown Prince Wilhelm's on the left. Behind this heavily fortified line was the Canal du Nord—in itself a serious obstacle. Beyond the Canal was Cambrai, the ultimate object of the whole operation. Cambrai was a railway centre from which supplies moved laterally to both great armies. It was behind the last strong line of defence, and defeat here would spell disaster to all the German armies.

Currie's task was therefore of first importance, and exceedingly difficult. The ground was pocked with old trenches, wire and shell-holes of past battles. The topography was tough, a series of valleys and hills with all the high points skilfully fortified. The Germans believed their positions impregnable, but the Canadians had taken other impregnable positions. The day before the attack the Germans paid their foe the supreme compliment by evacuating the town of Neuville-Vitasse at the tip of the Hindenburg Line. "The commitment of the Canadians, the best British troops, had been recognized," a German report states.

The attack was to start on August 26, and until his other divisions joined the Corps, the 51st Highland Division (British) was placed under Currie's command. A limited number of tanks (nine) had been assigned to each division but because of the difficulty of replacement, they were not to be used in advance of the infantry unless absolutely necessary. By daylight the tanks, waddling along in support, made good targets, and enemy artillery soon put many out of action.

There was no surprise this time, except for the early hour of attack—three a.m., almost a night operation. Caught somewhat off guard by the timing, the Germans were ready and waiting, with three divisions concentrated astride the River Scarpe. But the early start proved to be a great advantage.

Chapel Hill was taken early by the 4th Brigade, and the 8th Brigade captured Orange Hill, then made a clever circling movement around Monchy-le-Preux. But it was a lone lieutenant—Charles Smith Rutherford of the 5th C.M.R.'s—who, unaided, captured the ruined village of Monchy. Reconnoitring ahead of his assaulting troops, he approached a machine-gun pill-box unseen by the enemy, frightened them into surrendering, and compelled the German officer to call upon a second post further up the hill to surrender too. In all, he took two officers and forty-three men prisoner. When his men caught up with him they captured a third post with a further bag of thirty-five prisoners. To Lieutenant Rutherford went a Victoria Cross.

While here and there the enemy showed little stomach for battle, on the whole there was fierce resistance. By ten o'clock that night nearly all, and in some cases better than, the first objectives had been achieved. As before, the weight and skill of the artillery supported and protected the assaulting infantry in spite of uncut wire and enemy machine-gun fire.

But the operation had only begun. Bitter fighting lay ahead.

There had been showers during the first day and the following night it rained heavily so that the ground on the 27th was muddy and slippery. The Canadians had slowed down, troops tired, and replacements, the British 4th Division, failed to appear. By nightfall they had reached the enemy's first organized system of defence, the Fresnes-Rouvroy line.

The 28th was a day of desperately hard battles. The Sensée River was a serious obstacle and bloody struggles took place on its banks between the weary Canadians and fresh German divisions, rushed in to stem the tide. Here the 22nd Battalion again distinguished itself. Swimming the river, men engaged in hand-to-hand fighting, sometimes waist-deep in water. Twice they reached the opposite bank and were driven back, but the third time they made it, and along with the 24th Batallion, consolidated their position. Their casualties were appalling and included all their officers. Major Georges Vanier, later to become Governor General of Canada, lost his right leg at this time, and out of 600 men, only seventy came through uninjured. With all officers out of action and the ranks pitifully thinned, the medical officer, Dr. Albéric Marin, along to tend the wounded, saw the hesitation in those left, and springing forward, rallied and led the men on, till he in turn fell.

The two Canadian divisions were now exhausted; they had had three days of fierce fighting with little or no sleep. For a time the 3rd Division held a line nearly twice as long as its allotment. Relief came on the 29th, with the arrival of the 1st Division and the British 4th Division. The Independent Force, which had seen continual service, remained in the line protecting the flanks.

By the night of the 29th the Fresnes-Rouvroy line was, for the most part, in Canadian hands. By the 31st they were in full possession.

The Drocourt-Quéant Line, or D-Q as it was called, was the most heavily defended—the last organized system of defence. There were no illusions as to the cost of its capture—nor had the Germans illusions as to the cost of its loss, the ultimate defeat of the German armies.

In France, Britain and Canada, governments were apprehensive about the boldness of the offensive. After four years of war, it was hard to believe that the end was in sight. Even Sir Douglas Haig, that perennial optimist, told General Horne that if he had any doubts he could call off the campaign. But Currie was prepared and confident. The instinct of an experienced leader told him that the time was ripe to push on, and Foch agreed. More important, the Canadians, weary and depleted though they were, were in a high state of morale and exultation. The Jerries were on the run, and the will to fight and get it over with was strong in the whole Corps. Plans proceeded.

In the back areas sappers, pioneers, and railway troops worked on roads and rails. Supplies were maintained, and heavy artillery pounded the German defences. The D-Q Line, bisected by the Arras-Cambrai road, extended along crests or forward slopes of high ground, incorporating villages and dominating the attacking forces with observation and fire.

Currie's plan was to attack and cut the line at the critical point along the road, rolling back both enemy flanks. He hoped that once the D-Q Line was breached and crumbling, the advance could push right to, and over, the Canal du Nord. It was not to prove that easy.

There was plenty of fight left in the Germans, and fresh reinforcements in the shape of a crack Prussian regiment were rushed to the defence. On September 1 the enemy launched fierce counter-attacks against the 1st and 4th Divisions with temporary success. Counter-attacking themselves, the Canadians regained lost ground, but the Germans attacked again and intermittently during the night.

At five a.m. the next day, when the big drive started, elements of the 4th Division had been fighting almost continuously for twenty-four hours.

The early morning was dark and stormy. The opening bombardment was made to the accompaniment of thunder and lightning as General Morrison's great guns demolished rows of heavy wire, trenches, and support lines. As the Canadians surged forward, tanks and armoured cars cut through enemy defences, spraying the enemy with fire that should have been annihilating. But at breakthrough points the Germans were able to enfilade the attackers, while big guns picked off the tanks. Armoured cars, with their superior speed, got off more lightly, but hostile machine-guns and mortars poured punishing fire into the infantry.

The Canadians advanced nevertheless; the D-Q Line was taken but the battle was by no means won. The infantry was now beyond the range of artillery support, but within that of German rear guns. These made the most of their opportunity, stiffening enemy resistence, and the Canadians suffered accordingly.

In the day's fighting seven Victoria Crosses were awarded, two in the 16th Battalion. An American, Lance-Corporal W. H. Metcalf, received one, the commanding officer, Lieutenant-Colonel Cyrus Peck, the other. How many others were deserved but not witnessed is a matter for conjecture, for the Canadians fought with a ferocity and courage that overcame the desperate last-stand determination of the enemy.

While the Canal du Nord was not reached that day, the advance was up to five miles on a front of 7,000 yards and the strongest defence of the Hindenburg Line was taken. A few days later a British staff officer, walking over the area with a Canadian war correspondent remarked that "the position was impregnable had the Germans chosen to defend it." Granted enemy morale was waning, but the piles of German dead from seven divisions—among them regiments of the elite Guards Reserves—bore witness that the Germans *had* chosen to defend it, and in so doing had killed or wounded over 5,600 Canadians.

General Currie, in this action, paid special tribute to the 1st Division, and compared it as equal if not surpassing the victory at Amiens.

The Corps Commander's intentions for pressing the attack next day were foiled by the Germans, who on the night of the 2nd started to withdraw behind the Canal du Nord. The next two days the Canadians spent mopping up and making a general advance. The 2nd and 3rd Divisions came through, relieving the weary 1st and 4th, and occupying a line along the banks of the Canal du Nord.

The breaking of the hinge of the German defences had repercussions up and down the entire front, as the German High Command gave orders to withdraw. This meant abandoning all the ground won in their victorious offensive the previous spring, except to the immediate south where the British Third Army was still fighting stiff opposition in extensions of the Hindenburg Line.

From heights of land now in their possession the Canadians could see the lush fields of pastoral France, tall trees thick with foliage, seemingly tranquil villages, church spires piercing the skyline—few signs of the ravages of war.

They could also see in the foreground the east bank of the Canal du Nord, laced with wire and bristling with guns. Immediately behind, troops surged in confusion, and to the Canadian staff the temptation to press forward was great. But surprise was impossible, bridges had been destroyed, and the men were weary, their ranks depleted after the continual four weeks of fighting from August 8. Part of Currie's skill was in knowing when to stop, when to push on.

In his book *Canada's Hundred Days*, J. F. B. Livesay says that Currie was asked to attack over the canal to relieve pressure on the British Third Army, but refused on the grounds that it was a hopeless and needless sacrifice of his men. There were now twelve miles of captured territory to repair, guns and supplies to bring forward. Good generalship demanded the suspension of action, and that was what the Canadians had in full. The Germans, from excellent defensive positions, watched the preparations, indulging in desultory sniping and bombardment. By destroying the bridges and flooding the marshes, the enemy had cut themselves off from aggressive action, so the Canadians took their time, moving back out of machine-gun range. Here they re-organized, re-fitted, and rested to the extent conditions would permit.

Early in September General Foch presented his campaign plans to his commanders—a general attack on the whole front, from the sea southward to beyond Verdun on the River Meuse. It was to begin September 27. King Albert of the Belgians was to attack in Flanders; the British to the south against Cambrai and St. Quentin; the French at Mézières; and, at the far end of the line, the Americans, having already seen action at St. Mihiel, were allotted the Argonne-Meuse area.

General Haig made his plan and assigned to the Canadians the capture of Bourlon Wood, the protecting of the left flank of the British Third Army, and a general advance on Cambrai. But first the Canadians must cross the canal by frontal attack. This was the same task at which Currie had recently balked.

The canal was a formidable obstacle. The dominant position of the enemy on the opposite bank was ideal for defence, enabling them to enfilade all bridging efforts and attacking forces. General Currie, on principle, avoided frontal attacks wherever possible. In this situation he believed it would be murder. Faced with the problem, he made his own reconnaissance and presented a shrewd alternative plan to his superiors.

Beyond the southern boundary of the Corps' right flank—the other side of the Arras-Cambrai road—construction of the canal had been abandoned at the start of the war. Here the bed was dry and firm, and the distance from bank to bank was about forty yards. The troops would be able to cross at this point, but on such a narrow front that a large force must be squeezed in, defenceless in the process of crossing, and a superlative target for enemy guns.

This was the plan Sir Arthur presented to Sir Henry Horne. Withdraw the Corps from its present position unobtrusively, replacing it with the 56th Division of the British 22nd Corps; side-slip the Canadians to the south. Assembling the night before, the Corps, conforming to a narrow front of 2,700 yards, would cross swiftly under a covering barrage, while the engineers built crossings for the artillery and supply groups. Once across, the front would fan out to 9,700 yards or more, the 1st Division swinging left and north, along the bank where they could attack the German defences from the rear. Success here would permit crossing by the British troops.

With the 2nd Division remaining in reserve, the 4th and 3rd were to press on, the former attacking Bourlon Wood, a key-point of Geman defence, the latter fanning right to protect the flank of the Third Army. The role of the Third Army was to join with the 4th Division in encircling Bourlon Wood. Safely across the Canal du Nord, the whole front could advance on the Canal d'Escaut and Cambrai, as Haig's plan required.

The audacity of this scheme stunned the Higher Command. The risks were stupendous. If the Germans got wind of the intended crossing they could wipe out the whole Corps with little, if any, loss to themselves. Added to the humiliation and loss of British prestige would be the destruction of the Canadian Corps.

Sir Arthur Currie was fairly caught between the devil and the deep sea. He knew the risks involved, but he also knew that the frontal attack was certain destruction, with little hope of any success, beyond occupying the enemy while the British crossed. His plan, on the other hand, would at least give the Corps a chance, and bring closer the fruits of victory. He believed it to be feasible.

At a conference in mid-September the commanders pointed out all the objections and risks. Currie had considered them all. He countered by pointing out the risks and certain losses of the alternative. Finally he wrung uneasy assent. Then, disturbed by second thoughts, one by one they visited him at Corps Headquarters to question his wisdom; the Commander-in-Chief, the First Army Commander, the Third Army Commander.

Returning from his visit with Currie, General Horne said to his Major-General, General Staff, Hastings Anderson: "I don't believe I ought to let them do it!"

General Anderson replied: "If Currie says they can do it, they will!"

General Byng, too, was apprehensive. He read over the plan again, approving it in principle, but terming it the most difficult manoeuvre yet attempted on a battlefield in the war.

"Old man, do you think you can do it?" he asked doubtfully.

Currie believed he could. Writing later, he explains why.

"The operation called for the most skilful leadership on the part of the commanders, the highest state of discipline on the part of the troops."

These qualities were attributes of his Corps. While only success justified the risk, Sir Arthur had the courage and confidence to take it. Douglas Haig's confidence in Currie and his generalship is manifest by his acquiescence, for once more he had been warned by the British cabinet not to incur great losses. His reputation and prestige rested in Sir Arthur's hands.

By September 26 the 22nd Corps had replaced the Canadians in front of the strongly held German defences. By day, to an observer, there was little to be seen to the south, only the empty desolate wasteland of recent battles. But hidden in the maze of old German trenches and dugouts were thousands of men.

Night fell on the short September day of the 26th. As darkness screened them, men tumbled out of hiding and silently formed up for a twelve-mile diagonal march, forward and south, to the dry canal bed.

Up came the engineers, laden with steel and lumber, ready to start the vital bridging operations the moment the attack began. Batteries of artillery were in position. First an opening barrage, then once the men were across, the guns must follow up at the earliest moment the engineers made it possible.

Just after midnight heavy rain made the going difficult, but it cleared by four and the men had a meal and a tot of rum. At 5:20 a.m. the barrage opened and the crossing began—on a narrow two-battalion front. Almost at once the green flares of enemy s.o.s. signals lit the sky. But the surprise was complete, and there was comparatively little response from enemy guns.

Field batteries that had "tailed" the infantry took positions on the canal bank, covering men scrambling up the western slopes. By then the rear batteries had moved forward and were crossing bridges that the engineers had constructed under fire.

Once across, the operation went as planned. The Corps fanned out on a 9,700-yard front that soon extended to 15,000 yards. The 1st Division, bearing left along the east bank, surprised and routed the strong German line, enabling the British to cross and join in the fray.

The 4th Division attacked Bourlon Village and the Wood, but the

Third Army, expected on the right, was delayed by stiff opposition and did not arrive in time to help. In consequence the 3rd Division, protecting its flank, was held up too. Going it alone, with their right unprotected, the 4th had great difficulty in capturing the Wood—and then found themselves on a dangerous salient and subjected to enfilade fire from their right.

It was past nightfall before they reached their first objective, just beyond the Wood. Their casualties were heavy, and would have been greater but for the valour of two young lieutenants—G. T. Lyall of the 102nd Battalion and S. L. Honey, of the 78th Battalion—who, in separate actions, stormed and put out of action enemy strong-points that were holding up advances. Both men won Victoria Crosses, but Lieutenant Honey was killed.

For four days the attack pressed on towards Cambrai. Enemy resistance steadily increased as men came up against uncut wire dominated by machine-guns, and by September 30, casualties had reached serious proportions.

October 1 was perhaps, for the Canadians, the most discouraging day of the operation. Rain had made the roads slippery, which delayed dispatch riders and, consequently, orders. Casualties mounted with heartbreaking reverses as captured ground was recaptured in counter-attacks, and had to be captured again. Gains that day were hardly more than a mile, but the Canadians had been fighting for five consecutive days and most nights. Exhausted, with ranks depleted, they had engaged nine full German divisions and parts of three others. General Currie advised General Horne that their action must be broken off.

But the Corps commander's gamble had paid off in full. The Canal du Nord had been crossed with a minimum of casualties; the way had been cleared for the British 22nd Corps to cross; the 3rd Division had been able to protect the left flank of the Third Army in its difficult advance from the south. Cambrai was now besieged on three sides.

Anticipating further resistance, the Corps artillery put on a heavy barrage early in the morning of October 2, but all was quiet. For the time being the Germans had had enough. They were withdrawing, but the city was not decisively captured for another week.

Meanwhile operations on the other fronts had gone fairly well for the Allies. The enemy had been shifting their crack divisions up and down the line, desperately trying to cope with the many concerted attacks from the north to the south. The Americans, striking between the River Meuse and the Argonne Forest, took terrible punishment, for the seasoned German troops were fighting with a desperate ferocity—receiving, but also inflicting tremendous casualties. But for the enemy the writing was on the wall, even to the men in the ranks. The capture of Cambrai would smash the last German defence line and cut their armies in half.

A lull in the fighting gave the Canadian Corps a brief respite to catch their breath, but too much time would give the Germans a chance to catch theirs, and this must be avoided. So while the elements of the Corps rested, the artillery harassed the enemy and the Independent Force made forays into the enemy lines, disrupting any attempts at organized defence.

In the beleaguered city the Germans frantically withdrew all supplies they could handle. Huge fires indicated they were burning what they must leave.

The many canals through the region were obstacles to the advancing troops, for the Germans were destroying bridges. But until their withdrawal was complete, the bridges were as necessary to them as to the Allies. Here the engineers displayed outstanding courage and audacity in forestalling enemy demolitions. In one instance, Captain C. N. Mitchell ran across a bridge and, single-handed, fought off a party of Germans while his men removed charges and cut wires. He killed three of the enemy, captured twelve, and was awarded the Victoria Cross.

On October 8 the Canadians were again pressing forward. The night was dark and wet as the 2nd Division surprised the enemy northeast of the city, and crossed the Escaut Canal, with the batteries of Brutinel's Brigade covering their flank. The 17th Corps of the Third Army was supposed to sweep along the southeast of Cambrai and join with the 2nd Division in encircling the city, but they failed to arrive till late afternoon of the next day, so the Germans got away.

On the west, the 4th and 5th C.M.R. of the 3rd Division entered Cambrai to find it evacuated, except for small parties of Germans intent on total destruction. Fires were already raging, delayed-action booby-traps and mines were set. The Canadians turned their immediate attention to saving what they could of the ravaged and looted city, while the Independent Force pursued the enemy, cutting off large parties and destroying their defences.

Cambrai was in Canadian hands by October 9, but there was mopping up to do, centres of strong resistance to be broken, the canal to be cleared. The final action before the Corps moved on was the capture of the village of Iwuy. There the 2nd Division and the Independent Force fought a vicious little battle with a determined enemy. Ground was gained, lost, and regained again before the day was finished. Then the front was taken over by the British.

This Canadian army of four divisions had made an impressive record in forty-seven days. From August 28 to October 11, it advanced twenty-three miles, fought thirty-one German divisions, and liberated fifty-four towns in an area of 116 square miles. Any suggestion that enemy resistance had been desultory, or that the Germans lacked the will to fight, is repudiated by the casualty list—in all 30,806 Canadians dead, wounded and missing.

18

VALENCIENNES TO MONS

The same day the Corps took Cambrai, the Canadian Cavalry Brigade was employed to the southeast in their last and probably most successful operation of the war.

Operating with the 3rd Cavalry Division, the three regiments and a battery of Royal Canadian Horse Artillery charged through shell-fire and machine-gun bullets to capture enemy-held villages in the region of Le Cateau. This was cavalry country, and forays suited to that vanishing mode of combat took place.

They advanced eight miles on a three-mile front, forestalling enemy demolitions, and captured 400 prisoners—all for the cost of 168 casualties. But in an age of machinery and armour, war on the Western Front proved that horse-soldiers had no place in that kind of combat. It took twenty years for this to register, for as late as 1938, horses were still eating their heads off in military establishments.

In October, the First World War was won, but not over. Germany's allies, Bulgaria, Austria-Hungary, and Turkey signed armistices or were on the verge of doing so. Germany herself had approached President Wilson, but mistakenly believed that the greater resistance her armies offered, the better the conditions she could expect. Her forces were still in conquered country, still looting, demolishing, violating French villages.

October 14 brought a personal loss to veterans of the Corps. On that day Major-General L. J. Lipsett was killed by a sniper's bullet. General Lipsett had been with the Canadians from the start of the war when he organized the militia in Victoria, British Columbia. He had helped train and mould the Corps, but in September had been transferred back to the British army to command the British 4th Division. His death was sincerely mourned.

Still fighting vicious rearguard actions, the Germans retreated, with the Canadians in close pursuit. The canals and rivers continued to pose difficulties, and the Germans did a thorough job with road-blocks, mines, and booby-traps. But the pursuers surged forward with an exuberance that not even the rain, coming down in torrents, could dampen. Contact must be maintained and no respite permitted the enemy, so speed was essential. A squadron of cavalry and two batteries of Brutinel's Brigade were attached to both the 1st and 4th Divisions.

Soon the enemy was running so fast that he took no time to evacuate civilians or demolish their homes. Still, for the pursuers supplies were becoming a serious problem. The liberation of towns resulted in thousands of joyous but starving inhabitants begging food and throwing themselves on the liberators, kissing and embracing them. But there was no time to lose. Most of the men shared their rations, returned the kisses, and moved on to further towns and hearts to conquer.

The temper of the troops was changing and hardening. They were entering country that had been occupied for four long years and the desecration and desolation shocked and angered the Canadian soldiers. The Germans must have known their defeat was imminent, yet their retreat was marked by wanton viciousness against innocent and long-suffering civilians. Sometimes a village was smothered with gas bombs; all were looted and stripped of essentials and non-essentials. Industries were wrecked beyond repair, mine-shafts destroyed, livestock taken—even an old nanny goat on which a sick child's life depended. Grain that could not be taken away was scattered to the four winds before starving eyes.

In the village of Lewarde the enemy had converted a large barn into a concert hall and a talented German with sardonic humour had painted three murals. The first showed a slender woman plowing behind a huge ox; the second an aged man and small child sowing seed; the third a burly Boche reaping the harvest, silhouettes of armed soldiers on the skyline.

It was here that a load of village furniture, crated and labelled "by order of the Army Command," was captured on a siding. Villagers told how food, sent by missions of neutral countries, was commandeered by the soldiery.

By these acts alone, at a time when there was nothing to gain, the Germans lost any sympathy a defeated army might have aroused at the peace table. They gained instead the deep-rooted hatred of at least one generation.

At Denain, a sizable city not far from Valenciennes, the Germans took up battle positions, but they had lost too many guns for their artillery to be a problem. The 4th Division made short work of their rearguard action and swarmed into the town, battling isolated pockets of Germans while the main body fled on. Coinciding with the Canadians' entry was the arrival of the British 22nd Corps from the southwest.

The 1st Division, which had been battling continually for two weeks, was now relieved and went out of the line. Although they could not know it, their fighting days were over. Foch's spearhead was sharpening to a narrow front with the fast-moving point prodding deeply into the enemy's rear.

On went the chase. Each morning a test barrage was fired by the artillery to find out the enemy's reaction. If there was none, scouts went out to see why. It was becoming evident that the Germans were racing for Valenciennes, where the recurring Canal de l'Escaut could be flooded, an effective barrier for a last-stand defence.

The whole region was criss-crossed by irrigation canals. On the outskirts, southwest of Valenciennes, Mont Houy dominated the inundated plain, and here the Germans were strongly entrenched. Machine-guns and rows of wire lined the canal banks. The position was a strong one. Meanwhile, the Canadians were acutely in need of supplies. Currie ordered his troops to stabilize their line and await the arrival of the British, advancing from the south. The respite was welcome and might give time for the rations to catch up.

Attack was complicated. Strict orders had been issued against bombarding the city, hitherto spared, and still occupied by many French civilians. The Germans suffered no such restraint. Their artillery harassment made life uncomfortable and hazardous.

The flooded areas extended over many square miles. Tactically, the main attack must be made from the south against the heavily dominant feature, Mont Houy. After difficult fighting the British 22nd Corps forced their way to the south of this prominence and General Horne summoned General Currie to discuss the capture of Valenciennes. The resulting plan was a battle in three stages.

On October 28 the British 51st Highland Division would attack from the southwest and capture Mont Houy. This achieved, the Canadian 4th Division would then take over on the night of the 28th-29th, and press to the outskirts of the city. For the third stage, they must bear right and capture the high ground on the east, thereby outflanking the city and permitting the rest of the Canadian Corps to cross the canal and enter from the west.

It did not quite work out as hoped.

The Highlanders, although well supported by artillery, met unexpectedly strong opposition. They gained the hill, but a sharp counter-attack drove them back on the slope, objective unachieved. General Currie postponed Canadian relief twenty-four hours. General Horne's orders, issued that afternoon, re-affirmed that the Canadians were to proceed as ordered, provided the Highlanders' objective had been reached.

Consequently the tired 51st fought off counter-attacks all next day, and were relieved by the British 49th Division and the 10th Canadian Infantry Brigade. They renewed the assault with success on the 29th. Currie's decision later provoked criticism from the Major-General General Staff of the First Army, who held that the Canadian Commander quibbled. The Canadian relief should not have been postponed.

General McNaughton challenged this opinion, recalling a somewhat similar situation in 1916 at the battle for the St. Eloi Craters. Then the 2nd Divison, in their first major engagement, was ordered to take over in the middle of a deteriorating battle, suffered inordinately in appalling conditions, and received more blame than credit. Their commander, General Alderson, had been made the scapegoat. General McNaughton felt that this time Sir Arthur was justified, for it gave the Canadian heavy artillery "full and proper opportunity to do our work, free from the hysteria of a suddenly improvised attack."

The rest of the battle went as planned. It was here at Valenciennes that the Canadian artillery distinguished itself so markedly.

The city was to be spared as much as possible, but the industrial suburbs and steel works were crammed with German troops, and these were singled out for bombardment. From Mont Houy, now in Canadian hands, the artillery, by unique and clever disposition of guns, was able to cover Canadian attacks on both the west and south with a creeping barrage, and by oblique fire to enfilade the enemy's positions as well. Their superb counter-battery work silenced the enemy guns, and smoke shells screened the bridging units and the assaulting troops. Nothing could withstand the preponderance and skill of such gunfire, used to support the minimum number of men, the 10th Brigade. There was no wastage of manpower here.

The attack started before dawn on November 1. The enemy held out till the next day; they suffered tremendous losses and evacuated the city that night.

Skilful preparations and execution were responsible for the Allied success. German losses were exceptionally heavy—Canadians buried eight hundred of their dead, as against eighty of their own men killed. Before leaving, the Germans turned their batteries on the reservoirs and the power stations, cutting off water and light.

Refugees, going both ways, packed the roads along the route. The Germans had transported whole villages to other locations, it being easier to control the destitute. But the confusion and traffic jams seriously disrupted supply columns, particularly as there were now thousands of starving mouths to feed. There were wounded to get back too, although medical units had moved well forward. Victory was still costing lives and broken bodies.

Along the whole front, from the sea to Verdun, the Allies were advancing. As the Canadians pressed forward, it rained almost continuously. The terrain was difficult at best, laced with rivers, swamps and irrigation ditches. The rain made swift-running streams of the waterways, and without the engineers and railways troops all progress would have bogged down.

On November 6 the Belgian frontier was crossed. Small pockets of Germans were still resisting, but others were surrendering enthusiastically. The 4th Division was relieved by the 2nd, and for them too, the war was over.

On the right, enemy resistance had forced the 22nd Corps to give ground, and on the left the 8th Corps had been unable to cross the Scheldt Canal, so the Canadians had to look well to both their flanks as the spearhead neared the heart of Mons. Here in Belgium there was little evidence of destruction. According to reports of some war correspondents, the Belgians were not as friendly as the French, and in some instances expressed sympathy for the defeated Germans. Obviously, the Boche had pursued a very different line in Belgium.

Rumours of an armistice had been flying thick and fast, but rumours were always present, and men had learned to discount or disregard them. On Sunday, November 10, the Canadians were on the outskirts of Mons. With his guns positioned east of the city, the enemy kept up a heavy barrage and harassing machine-gun fire as the Canadians approached. The Germans who fought at all, did so with a fierce desperation to kill or be killed before the war ended.

The Royal Canadian Regiment now relieved the weary P.P.C.L.I. who had been marching and fighting almost continuously. With the 42nd Battalion (Royal Highlanders of Canada) they prepared to attack Mons that day, but as usual, canals and ancient moats around the city hampered their advance and enemy resistance was strong. Attack by daylight was rash and pointless. They postponed action until early morning. Behind the city the enemy could be seen massing for attack—or possibly withdrawal. Artillery fire soon broke them up, but Corps Headquarters expressly forbade shelling Mons itself, even in the face of hostile fire.

As night fell, a heavy barrage came down on the R.C.R. and the Highlanders, under which the enemy began to retire out of the city. By eleven p.m. patrols from both regiments reported that the city was evacuated, and our troops lost no time. They crossed the canal, and in the small hours of the morning of November 11 were in possession of the city. Only one company of Germans was left to resist, and the Canadians made short work of them. Soon every citizen was out of bed and on the streets rejoicing.

At dawn, as outposts were relieved, a rumour spread that there was to be no advance that day. A little later, Brigade Headquarters received the message: "Hostilities will cease at 11:00 a.m., November 11th. Troops will stand fast on the line reached at that time, which will be reported to Divisional Headquarters immediately. Defensive precautions will be maintained. There will be no intercourse with the enemy of any description."

Sceptical and unbelieving, the troops hung on to their steel helmets and their gas masks.

At eleven a.m. that Monday morning, crowds filled the city square. The pipers of the Royal Highlanders of Canada led the march past, and the Mayor presented the keys of the city to Brigadier General J. A. Clark, commanding the 7th Brigade. Still on the ground lay bodies of German soldiers, killed earlier, and the inhabitants of Mons kicked them where they lay.

Sir Douglas Haig's last communiqué stated: "Canadian troops of the First Army have captured Mons."

For the troops it was an anticlimax. For the most part, their reaction was quiet and subdued.

The capture of Mons brought the war back full circle. Here on a Sunday in August 1914, the British fought their first engagement of the war and were defeated, and the humiliating Allied retreat began. Nearby the 3rd Division sector was a British regiment, the 5th Lancers, which had taken part in the first battle. With it were men who had survived that action, only to die on the same battlefield four years later. On November 11, only one Canadian was killed at Mons.

That afternoon, Currie signed the Golden Book of Remembrance at the City Hall. Later, as he and his chief administrative officer and close friend, Brigadier General G. J. Farmar, surveyed the scene, General Farmar turned to his chief and said: "You know, General, the last time I was on this spot was in August, 1914."

"Well George," replied Sir Arthur, "it's taken a damned long time to get you back!"

19

THE CANADIANS CROSS THE RHINE AND THE CORPS COMMANDER COMES HOME

The fighting war was over. It was now up to the politicians.

In other theatres of conflict the enemy had submitted. Germany was the last to do so, but once it was apparent that hostilities threatened her own territory, the Imperial German Command sued for an armistice. The Canadian penetration had been dangerously deep.

On Sunday, November 10, the President of France made an official entry into Valenciennes. The Prince of Wales, Prince Arthur of Connaught, and Sir Arthur Currie were all present. President Poincaré praised the Canadians, saying: "They have shed their blood freely for France." The bands played "O Canada."

In Mons a week later a similar celebration took place—the Prince of Wales and the army chiefs present. A gold medal was struck bearing the inscription: *"La Ville de Mons au Lieut-général Sir Arthur Currie, en souvenir de la liberation de la cité pars le Corps Canadien."* The carillon played "O Canada." Days later Albert, King of the Belgians, made his state entry into the city and congratulated Sir Arthur on the achievements of the Canadian Corps, "unsurpassed by any Corps in Europe." By this time "O Canada" was a well-hummed tune in those parts of France and Belgium, and the natives probably knew the words better than the Canucks themselves.

The destruction of rails and roads made supply a most difficult problem, so the 3rd and 4th Divisions remained in Belgium while the 1st and 2nd had the honour of marching to the Rhine, 170 miles away.

They moved off on November 18. En route were signs of occupation, nothing like the devastation seen in France, but food was scarce. At first, army horses developed a startling propensity for getting "lost"—to be found in the back sheds of local butchers, or regrettably, in the shops themselves. Learning the hard way, the horse-soldiers thereafter kept close watch on their mounts.

By December 4 the frontier was reached, but there were only a few surly Germans to witness the triumphal crossing. In Germany there was no devastation. According to some war correspondents, in contrast to Belgium, food seemed plentiful, in the countryside at least, although other sources reported the Germans were starving.

The victory march was no sinecure. For the most part the weather was foul; cobblestones, mud, and steeply wooded hills made the going about as tough as it could be. Billets were poor or non-existent. Frequently the rations failed to turn up, and food was a problem for man and beast. Drivers took bill-hooks or borrowed scythes to cut forage for their horses, and too often men marched off in the morning breakfastless.

They had reached the Rhine the second week in December, and the soldiers set about cleaning equipment, grooming their horses, tending blistered feet and patching their worn boots. Throughout the march the Canadians had maintained the highest standard of discipline, for Currie was determined that they must, as he told them, "continue to be and appear to be, that powerful hitting force which has won the fear and respect of your foes, and the admiration of the world." This they did.

On December 13 the 1st Division crossed the Rhine at Cologne, where Sir Hubert Plumer took the salute. On the same day the 2nd Division crossed at Bonn, Sir Arthur Currie taking the salute from the eighteen-mile column. Flags flying, brass and pipe bands playing, bayonets fixed and heads high, they marched across the Rhine, justifiably proud of themselves and their Corps.

Currie, surrounded by his staff, was deeply moved. This was the first ceremonial parade of his command—the tenacious desciplined army he had built and fought so stubbornly to maintain. Impulsively he touched the arm of General Brutinel nearby, saying softly: "I never realized till today, Bruty, what an irresistible force they are. There is nothing so impressive and so powerful anywhere!"

Among those not present to take part in the official Rhine crossing was the Independent Force. Still in their role as trouble-shooters, the Motors had gone ahead to deal with bands of Bolsheviks who were pillaging and terrorizing the countryside. Disorganized by defeat and forbidden to carry weapons, the civil authorities were helpless to deal with the terrorists. Answering a plea for help, the Motor Machine Gun Brigade sped forward to protect the local inhabitants and bring about order.

Near Bonn an armed gang was besieging the castle of the Kaiser's sister, Princess Louise, at Friesdorf. At the height of the trouble an errant officer of the Motors, absent on duty when his battery left Mons, arrived in Bonn, having hitch-hiked his way there by various means. Authorizing the burgomaster to arm the police and auxiliaries, he led the small force against the revolutionaries. When the Motors arrived the next day, he gleefully boasted that he had attended to the whole matter.

The Canadians did not remain long in Germany. Transferred to Belgium, then to France, it was nearly summer before they were back in Britain, in embarkation camps awaiting transport home. In those months of waiting the good name of Canadian soldiers was sullied by a series of riots between November and June. Injuries, deaths and considerable destruction of property resulted in the three worst affairs, all brought on by small groups of agitators, bored or disgruntled at not getting back to Canada sooner.

War correspondents maintained these shameful incidents were never traced to the fighting troops of Canada. "Canadian fighting troops remained good soldiers until they ceased to be soldiers," wrote one reporter. "Those who attempted to give Canada a bad name were never those who helped give the country a good name," wrote another.

In August, 1919, Sir Arthur Currie returned to Canada to find he was without honour in his own country. Arriving in Halifax on a Sunday morning, he found a guard of honour and a few dignitaries on hand to make it official, but no welcoming crowd. In Ottawa, on Parliament Hill, Sir George Foster, acting Prime Minister, welcomed him home in almost dead silence, broken here and there by hisses from the small crowd of spectators. Currie maintained a stolid composure.

If he was torn to pieces within, he denied his enemies the satisfaction of witnessing his anguish.

But with dignity and restraint, he sought a place in history for his Corps. Addressing the Ottawa Canadian Club shortly after his return, he recounted their achievements.

"In the last hundred days," he said, "The Canadian Corps met and decisively defeated forty-seven different German Divisions. Of these forty-seven, we re-engaged seventeen that had been pulled out of the line and rested, making a grand total of sixty-four fresh divisions."

He was understandably proud of his Corps, but according to Stonewall Jackson: "Even a professional army is what its commander makes it. Its character sooner or later becomes the reflex of his own. . . . The history of famous armies is the history of great generals, for no army ever achieved great things unless it has been well commanded."

General Currie had many differences with the British Higher Command during his eighteen months as Corps commander. He refused to serve under General Gough, whom he considered incompetent. He protested against the Passchendaele action, agreeing to participate with his whole Corps or not at all. Then he picked his own date for attack, insisting on time to repair back areas and bring up supplies; and he refused to be hurried, for such details were the difference between defeat and victory.

In March, 1918, during a thirty-six-hour absence, his Corps was torn apart, separate divisions sent careering up and down the line. Only his return prevented their commitment to the sausage machine of the German advance, with the same hysterical lack of direction the British troops were enduring. His insistence on their return to his command incurred Haig's anger, but his Motor Machine Gun Brigade went in—cool, hard-hitting mobile batteries, trained to act independently. Their participation was valuable not only for their tremendous fire-power and field of movement, but for the confidence and leadership they gave to disorganized groups of men left leaderless by the hasty departure of their headquarters.

In August 1918 Currie was a strong force behind the great push at Amiens and the decision to transfer to Arras when the German defence stiffened. At the Canal du Nord, he refused to make a suicidal frontal attack, but his alternative plan showed a skill and courage incomprehensible to many of the other generals and saved the Canadian Corps from probable destruction.

Lastly, at Mont Houy he refused to inherit, at a moment's notice, a losing battle he had neither planned nor prepared for. Taking over a day later, the Canadians took Valenciennes with brilliant artillery tactics and a minimum of casualties.

At the end of the war Sir Arthur was high in the esteem and hearts of many British commanders. Horne, Plumer, Byng, Sir Douglas Haig, all regarded him with great respect and genuine affection. Even Gough had good words to say of him. The British officers who served in the Corps remained close friends for the rest of his life. To the French and Belgians he was a hero, and the high regard of the Generalissimo goes without saying. Foch had selected the Corps to spearhead his whole attack, and he listened with respect to Currie's opinions.

Only in Canada was General Currie disparaged, his greatness unacknowledged. Colonel Nicholson's fine history of the Canadians in World War I was not published till 1962, seven years after that of World War II. Two generations grew up ignorant of the feats of the Canadian Corps and their commander. The detractors of Currie did a thorough job. Today he is almost forgotten, a vague memory of doubtful ability.

For a short time he served as Inspector General of Militia, then became Principal and Vice-Chancellor of McGill University in Montreal, where he was loved and respected. He died in 1933, still tormented by false allegations. Today there is no national recognition or tribute to this great Canadian soldier. He has indeed faded away.

20

1919: PEACE ON EARTH

At war's end the Canadian Corps numbered approximately 150,000 men. Casualties in the four years of fighting totalled 212,288, more than 52,000 of them fatal. But the Corps did not represent all the Canadians who took part in the First World War. Apart from those who fought in the British services, there were those in the Royal Flying Corps, the Canadian Navy, medical units, engineers, bridging groups and tunnelling companies, some of whom served in the Middle East and Russia. Over 22,000 Forestry Troops worked in the British Isles and France. Nearly 20,000 Railway Troops, suffering better than 10 per cent casualties, and the oft-mentioned Canadian Cavalry Brigade both served under fire, frequently under General Currie's command, and always distinguished themselves with great courage.

In Bonn, General Brutinel remained for a short time with his Machine Gunners, then a new task was assigned him. He set to work compiling war diaries of staff officers of all Canadian formations for the year 1918, with emphasis on the last one hundred days of battle. The summer found him in Paris, attached to the British Mission when the Peace Treaty was being drafted at the Hotel Majestic. It was there that Sir Robert Borden, on a visit to the Mission, persuaded the General to become a British subject. He received naturalization papers in 1919, after his return to Canada. Urged by Sir Arthur Currie, Brutinel accepted the appointment of military historian in the War Narrative Section of the Army.

But a year later General Brutinel returned to France. He was loath to go, for he loved Canada and Canadians, but personal factors forced his departure and Canada was the loser. He retained his membership in the Canadian Institute of Mines and Metallurgy, becoming a life member in 1925, a member of the Fifty Years Club of the Institute in 1961. To the day of his death at the age of eighty-two on September 21, 1964, he hoped to see the Canadian Corps and its commander take an honoured place in history.

In 1959 surviving machine-gunners in Canada erected a bronze plaque in the Chateau Laurier Hotel in Ottawa where the 1st Canadian Automobile Machine Gun Brigade had its beginning. It hangs in the east entrance of the main foyer. The general was not well enough to come to Canada, and it was unveiled by his daughter Raymonde, Mme. Paul Robert, who lives in Montreal. It is roughly twenty by forty inches in size. At the top is a portrait of Brutinel in bas-relief with replicas of the Corps badge on either side—a crown over crossed gun-barrels. Underneath it reads:

CANADIAN MACHINE GUN CORPS
COMMANDED BY
BRIG. GEN. R. BRUTINEL, C.B., C.M.G., D.S.O.

Below this is a pockmarked battlefield showing machine-gun crews manning their guns, and beneath that again is the text:

CANADIAN MACHINE GUNS ON VIMY RIDGE
IN MEMORY
OF THE MEMBERS OF

THE CANADIAN MACHINE GUN CORPS
WHO DIED ON ACTIVE SERVICE
AND IN HONOUR OF
THOSE WHO SERVED
1914-1919

A smaller plaque underneath explains:

IN THE CHATEAU LAURIER THE
CANADIAN MACHINE GUN CORPS HAD
ITS BEGINNINGS. HERE, IN AUGUST 1914
MAJOR RAYMOND BRUTINEL
ENROLLED THE FIRST RECRUITS
FOR THE CORPS.

By autumn, 1919, the demobilization of the Canadian Corps was complete, but men returned to a changed world. Strikes, crime, prohibition, rum-running and its condoned lawlessness, pacifism and a Russian import, Bolshevism, dominated the peaceful world. The old way of life, for which men had fought, was gone, never to return.

Having fought a war to end war, those who were left of the citizen-soldiers returned to civilian life, resuming their former professions and trades. Some of the school boys went back to school or university. A few joined the regular army as professional soldiers.

Two infantry regiments with proud battle honours were incorporated into the small permanent force—Princess Patricia's Canadian Light Infantry and the Royal 22nd Regiment, affectionately known as the Van Doos. A Royal Canadian Machine Gun Battalion survived for a few postwar years as regulars, horses replacing their motors, then was disbanded in 1922. One armoured car was returned to Canada to take its place in the National War Museum at Ottawa, but years later was claimed by the Royal Canadian Armoured Corps as a legitimate ancestor. The old vehicle, still mobile for ceremonial parades, spends periods at the R.C.A.C. School at Camp Borden on loan from the National War Museum.

And the Militia?

Sometimes despised by types in the Permanent Force, frequently ridiculed by pacifist-minded civilians, always an irritation to a parsimonious government, a hard core of veterans supported the Militia, contributing their meagre pay to keeping alive its great spirit. Twenty years later, in 1939, they again offered themselves and their sons for the defence of their country.

bibliography

GENERAL SIR ARTHUR CURRIE, *The Currie Papers* (private papers in the Dominion Archives, Ottawa)

BRIGADIER GENERAL RAYMOND BRUTINEL, *Recollections* (unpublished transcripts of tape recordings)

G. W. L. NICHOLSON, *Canadian Expeditionary Force, 1914-1919* (Official Canadian History), Ottawa, 1962

Canada in the Great War—6 volumes. Published from 1917-21 by "Various Authorities," mostly Canadian war correspondents.

SIR C. P. LUCAS, (ed.) *The Empire at War*, Volume II, "The Canadian Forces in the War," by F. H. Underhill. London: Humphrey Milford, 1921-23.

The Canadian Defence Quarterly, articles by General A. G. L. McNaughton (Vol. VI, no. 2, Jan. 1929) and Colonel Wilfred Bovey (Vol. XI, no. 2, Jan. 1934).

Canada, House of Commons Debates, Spring 1919.

BRIGADIER GENERAL S. L. A. MARSHALL, *The American Heritage History of World War I.* New York: American Heritage Publishing Co., 1964.

H. M. URQUHART, *Arthur Currie: The Biography of a Great Canadian.* Toronto: J. M. Dent, 1950.

J. F. B. LIVESAY, *Canada's Hundred Days.* Toronto: Thomas Allen, 1919.

GEORGE F. G. STANLEY, *Canada's Soldiers.* (Revised edition) Toronto: The Macmillan Co. of Canada, 1960.

J. F. C. FULLER, *Memoirs of an Unconventional Soldier.* London: Hutchinson, 1936.

LIEUTENANT COLONEL C. S. GRAFTON, *The Canadian "Emma Gees," a History of the Canadian Machine Gun Corps.* Ontario: Canadian Machine Gun Association, 1935.

JOHN TERRAINE, *Douglas Haig, The Educated Soldier.* London: Hutchinson. 1963.

ROBERT BLAKE (ed.), *The Private Papers of Douglas Haig, 1914-1919.* London: Eyre and Spottiswoode, 1952.

ALAN CLARKE, *The Donkeys.* London: Hutchinson, 1961.

CORRELLI BARNETT, *The Swordbearers.* London: Eyre and Spottiswoode, 1963.

LEON WOLFF, *In Flanders Fields.* New York: Viking Press, 1958.

DAVID DIVINE, *The Blunted Sword.* London: Hutchinson, 1964.

SIR MAX AITKEN, *Canada in Flanders.* London: Hodder and Stoughton, 1916.

BRIGADIER GENERAL C. BALLARD, *Smith-Dorrien.* London: Constable and Sons, 1931.

index